First Edition

Published by:
Untamed Mainer, LLC
PO Box 109
Little Deer Isle, ME 04650, USA
UntamedMainer.com

Cover Design: Angela Quintal-Snowman

Printed in USA

MAINE LIGHTHOUSES

The People, Histories, and Stories Connected to Them

Southern Maine Region

by Angela Quintal-Snowman

UNTAMED MAINER LLC
Little Deer Isle, Maine, USA

For my incredible children,
Aja and Treben,
who have always been beacons of light in my life.

"*Some of the most picturesque light-stations in the United States lighthouse establishment are on the rocks and islands off the coast of Maine. The ever-surging ocean; the fissured granite, seaweed-stained and tide-marked; the overhanging pines, gnarled and wind-whipped into fantastic shapes, impart a wild beauty to these sites. The towers which stand thereon are among our oldest coast lights, are built of granite and the hard gray of which has been softly darkened by age, and are of the old-fashioned type which the lover of the sea always associates with the idea of a lighthouse. Raising with an antique grace from among their picturesque environs, they seem peculiarly fitted to shed their light like a benediction upon the waves.*"

– Gustav Kobbé, 1897

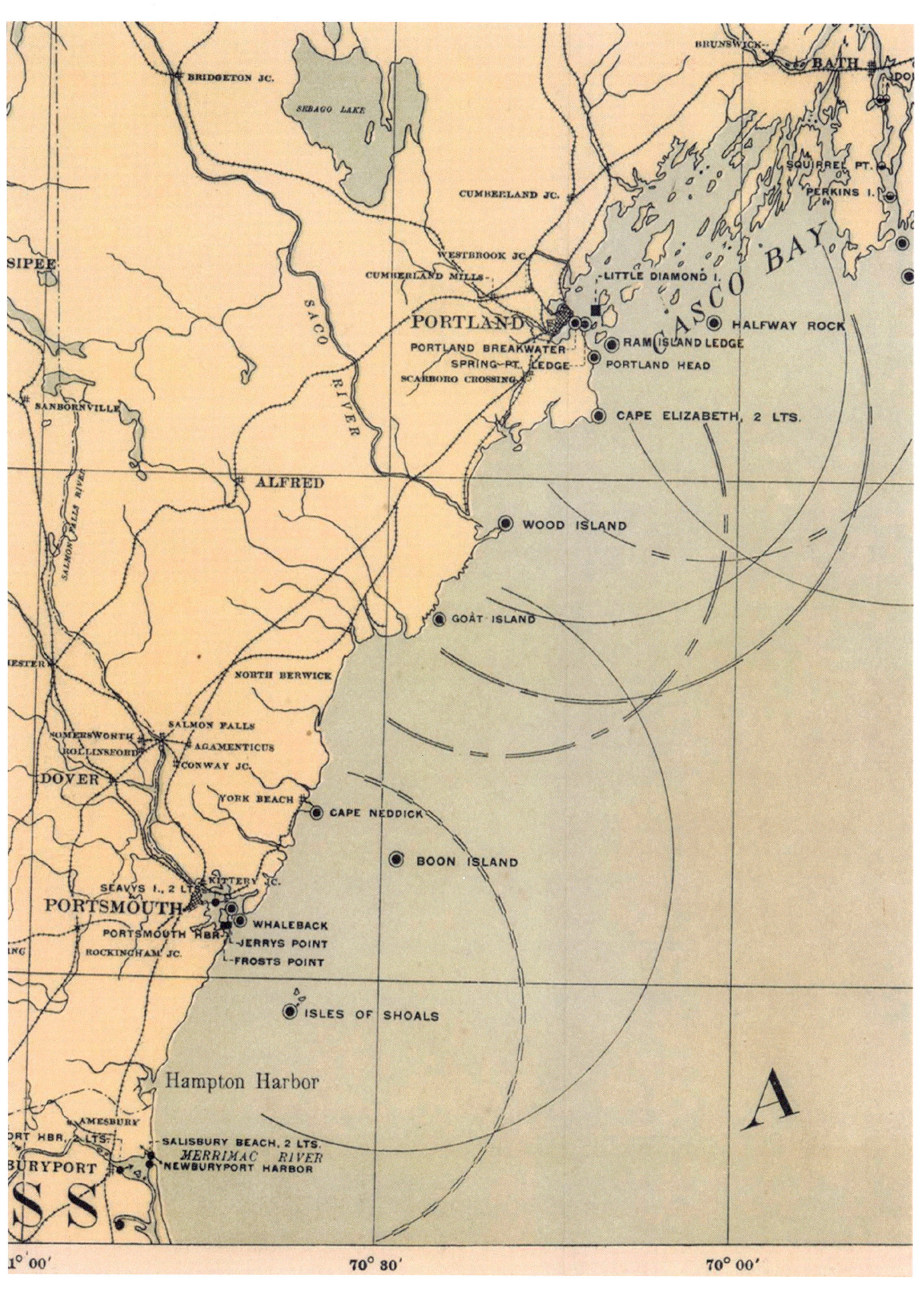

BRIDGTON JC.

SEBAGO LAKE

SIPEE

BRUNSWICK

BATH

DO

SQUIRREL PT.

PERKINS I.

CUMBERLAND JC.

WESTBROOK JC.

CUMBERLAND MILLS

LITTLE DIAMOND I.

CASCO BAY

SACO RIVER

PORTLAND

HALFWAY ROCK

PORTLAND BREAKWATER
SPRING PT. LEDGE
SCARBORO CROSSING

RAM ISLAND LEDGE

PORTLAND HEAD

SANBORNVILLE

CAPE ELIZABETH, 2 LTS.

SALMON FALLS RIVER

ALFRED

WOOD ISLAND

ESTER

NORTH BERWICK

GOAT ISLAND

SOMERSWORTH
ROLLINSFORD

SALMON FALLS
AGAMENTICUS
CONWAY JC.

DOVER

YORK BEACH

CAPE NEDDICK

BOON ISLAND

SEAVYS I., 2 LTS.
KITTERY JC.

PORTSMOUTH

WHALEBACK

PORTSMOUTH HBR.
ROCKINGHAM JC.

JERRYS POINT

FROSTS POINT

ING

ISLES OF SHOALS

Hampton Harbor

A

AMESBURY

RT HBR., 2 LTS.

BURYPORT

SALISBURY BEACH, 2 LTS.
MERRIMAC RIVER
NEWBURYPORT HARBOR

SS.

1° 00'

70° 30'

70° 00'

HOW THIS BOOK WAS WRITTEN

Dates

In researching dates there are often a lot of discrepancies. Although records were kept of most activities, they were mainly written by hand, and some people's handwriting wasn't as clear as others. I have used the most reliable sources I could find to write this book, and have done my best to provide the most accurate and likely dates when I encounter a discrepancy based on extensive research and historical knowledge.

Many dates, especially for lightkeeper appointments, look like this: (c. 1932). The "c." stands for "circa" and means around or approximately. This means precise records are unavailable and the date is a best estimate. If a date appears with a space before or after it like this: (1932-) or (-1932), it means one date could be verified but the other date could not be found or verified.

Keepers who I discovered died while working at a lighthouse are noted after their date(s) of service. ***Women keepers' names are in bold*** since there were so few employed in the Lighthouse Service.

Measurements

There is often conflicting information about measurements, especially height and distance. You'll find this even today when looking at the height of mountains or waterfalls when comparing multiple reliable maps and print sources. I used the most likely measurements based on information from multiple reliable sources when listing these numbers.

Spelling and Grammar Errors

Spelling and grammar errors found in direct quotes have been left exactly as they were written. Spelling and grammar errors in the rest of the text were accidentally overlooked by me personally, since I edited the book. I would be more than appreciative if you pointed them out to me so I can correct them for future editions!

Writing Style and Sources

This book is written as a guide with facts about Maine lighthouses accompanied by the historical stories that surround them, not a reference book. Because of this, I did not include direct references at the end of every paragraph and pages of endnotes referencing the location of every source I gathered my information from. Instead, I have included a list of references I used at the end of this book. If no state is listed after a town name, it is in Maine.

Photographs

Many older photographs have an unknown photographer's name, and the source or collection they came from is listed instead. Photograph dates were not always recorded. When no date is known, you will see the abbreviation "n.d." after the photograph description. I am a writer, not a photographer, which means all current photos were taken by professionals from Maine and all over the world who have visited this state and were captivated by these beautiful beacons of light. Photo credit abbreviations are spelled out in Appendix A.

CONTENTS

PART 1- INTRODUCTION TO MAINE LIGHTHOUSES

PART 2- MAINE LIGHTHOUSES

Notes after established dates: Lighthouses participating in the Maine Open Lighthouse Day are noted with a (K) if the keeper's house is open, a (T) if the tower is open, or a (KT) if both are open to the public. Lighthouses with a (D) were demolished and are no longer there.

PART 3- APPENDICES

LIGHTHOUSE HISTORICAL TIMELINE

1789 The First United States Congress passed the Lighthouses Act on August 7

1791 Maine's first lighthouse was finished, Portland Head Light

1820 Maine separates from Massachusetts and becomes a state

1852 The U.S. Light-House Board is established on August 31

1910 U.S. Bureau of Lighthouses is established to replace the Light-House Board, on July 1

1939 The Coast Guard assumes responsibility for the nation's lighthouses

1988 National Lighthouse Day was enacted by President Ronald Regan, annually celebrated on August 7th

1989 The 1st National Lighthouse Day was celebrated, marking the 200th anniversary of the Lighthouses Act

1996 The Maine Lights Program is established on October 16

2000 National Historic Lighthouse Preservation Act was signed

2008 Maine Open Lighthouse Day was established

HOW LIGHTHOUSES WERE BUILT, GOVERNED, AND MANAGED THROUGH THE YEARS

EARLY ADMINISTRATION & THE LIGHTHOUSES ACT (LIGHTHOUSE ESTABLISHMENT)

New England's first lighthouses were constructed and governed by regional colonies to aid in navigation along the rocky coast. Their construction and maintenance were supported through duties collected by individual states from merchant ships docking at nearby ports. In 1789, the recently formed federal government (1787) assumed responsibility for all previously established colonial lighthouses under the Lighthouses Act, passed by the First Congress, creating the Lighthouse Establishment.

The Lighthouse Establishment served to regulate and improve shipping trade routes and commerce for the new nation, granted federal control over lighthouse administration, and provided funding for the upkeep of current lighthouses and the construction of new stations. It is interesting to note that the original Lighthouses Act document became a lost part of the nation's history, as it never reached the National Archives, where all early Senate records were transferred to in 1937. Senate records had been moved to several locations starting in 1789, and it is unclear where the Lighthouses Act document ended up other than in private hands at some point. It wasn't until 1991, over two centuries later, that the original Lighthouses Act document was discovered in a manuscript dealer's collection, and the historical document was returned to its rightful place in the National Archives.

In the early years of the Lighthouse Establishment, President Washington personally approved all decisions regarding the administration of the nation's lighthouses. This included the approval of constructing Maine's first lighthouse, Portland Head Light, in 1791, which became the nation's first lighthouse completed under the Lighthouses Act. President Washington was also responsible for appointing lightkeepers to stations, a decision which was often based on military rank and service and personal relationships with the president.

LOCAL SUPERINTENDENCE

While lighthouse construction and appointment of keepers were decided by the federal government, the responsibility of supervising the construction, maintenance, and operation of lighthouses went to the local Collector of Customs. Their duties included choosing new sites to build lighthouses and purchasing the land, supervising the contractors who built the lighthouses, and authorizing repairs to lighthouse stations.

All major ports along the coast had a Collector of Customs who collected revenues from ships that used the ports for commerce. While Maine was still part of Massachusetts that responsibility went to the collector in Boston, who was Revolutionary War General Benjamin Lincoln, who held the post until 1809. He was replaced by Henry Dearborn, who held the position until 1812, then his son, Alexander Scammell Dearborn, took over until 1820 when Maine became an independent state.

After the separation from Massachusetts, it was recommended that the care and superintendence of Maine's lighthouses be transferred to Isaac Ilsley, Collector of Customs for the port of Portland, who assumed the duties on June 7, 1820. That same year, in response to a rapidly growing nation, President Monroe ordered the "care and superintendence of the lighthouse establishment" be transferred from the federal government to the Fifth Auditor of the Treasury, who was Stephen Pleasonton. Pleasonton remained in this position for 32 years, serving through nine presidencies. At the beginning of his appointment in 1820, the United States had 55 lighthouses, eight of which were located in Maine. At the end of his time in the position in 1852, the United States had 325 lighthouses, with 35 of them located in Maine.

EARLY LIGHTHOUSE CONSTRUCTION

Construction of early lighthouses was often shoddy. It was policy for the government to automatically accept the lowest bid received on lighthouse construction contracts, regardless of the bidder's skills and abilities. This meant that contractors with absolutely no building experience could win a contract, which they often did. This is evident in the high number of early lighthouses that needed to be rebuilt, some within just years of being completed.

These lighthouses were constructed from local materials that were easily accessible, including rubblestone and wood, using beach sand mixed with lime and saltwater as mortar. The lantern room was often constructed of iron and housed lanterns burning whale oil hung from a chandelier and surrounded by a series of curved reflectors to project and direct the beams of light. Wooden towers were prone to burning down or simply could not withstand the force of ocean waves during major storms, and therefore no early wooden towers built in Maine survived. Early masonry towers were prone to cracks and leaking due to the use of low-grade mortar that eroded with every storm wave that crashed into the lighthouse.

Winslow Lewis Patented Lamps & Reflectors
Mariners who traveled to and from Europe constantly complained about United States lighthouses and their system of lamps and reflectors, which was not as bright and didn't project as far as the systems used on the European coast. The United States used two variations of lamps and reflectors, one designed by Ami Argand of Europe, and the other by Winslow Lewis of the United States. A majority of Maine lighthouses used Winslow Lewis's patented lamps and reflectors.

Winslow Lewis, n.d., NA.

4

One of the biggest opponents to the use of Winslow Lewis's design was his own nephew, I.W.P. Lewis, who was a civil engineer and lighthouse station inspector. In a letter dated February 28, 1842, I.W.P. Lewis states that the United States had been using the Lewis lantern system since 1812, which was designed by a person who "was not a scientific man, nor had he any knowledge of optics whatever." Many letters were written by both uncle and nephew arguing their points regarding lighthouse illumination to Congress throughout the years. Winslow Lewis originally sold the patent for his lamps and reflectors system to the government for $20 and was thereafter contracted to install his illumination system in the lighthouses, giving him a vested interest in the United State's continued use of his design. I.W.P. Lewis was more interested in the progression and improvement of the Lighthouse Establishment and constantly petitioned to upgrade to newer, more effective systems.

In his 1842 letter to Congress, I.W.P. Lewis continues his argument that not only are United States lighthouses using inferior lighting compared to European methods, but that the construction of the lighthouses is not done by architects or engineers, and the inspection of the lighthouses, if any, is often done by incompetent men. Lewis also notes that the entire system of establishing and maintaining lighthouses is a "defective system," and therefore, it was necessary to appropriate a large sum of funds every year "to keep these wretched structures in habitable order."

His letter concludes with a proposed bill for "the better organization of the Lighthouse Establishment of the United States" by dividing the coast into four districts and employing engineers and architects to oversee the construction, inspection, and maintenance of all lighthouses. Lewis also called for the use of a newer lighting apparatus system in all lighthouses which was already in use in France and other lighthouses along the European coastline.

By 1851, the letter from I.W.P. Lewis, along with a growing number of written complaints from mariners, was finally addressed by Congress, who assembled a board to assess the state of the nation's lighthouses and the Lighthouse Establishment. The board discovered that many lighthouses were not tall enough to project their light far enough for mariners to see, and some were too close together to be able to tell the individual lighthouses apart. Both mariners and I.W.P. Lewis attributed the issue with the lights to the United States still using the outdated Winslow Lewis lamps and reflectors system.

The United States Light-House Board (USLHB)

In response to the information gathered from the assessment board, and to address the growing number of issues with the nation's lighthouses, Congress decided to revamp the entire system and replace Stephen Pleasonton, who had overseen the establishment for 32 years, with a group of nine members. In 1852, the United States Light-House Board was established, composed of three officers from the Navy, three officers from the Army, two highly educated civilian scientists, and the Secretary of the Treasury.

The Board established 12 districts to govern lighthouses, with the first district covering the coasts of Maine and New Hampshire. The Light-House Board focused on quality over price and restored or rebuilt many stations upon taking charge, and replaced the cheaper Winslow Lewis lamps and reflectors optics with the more efficient and much brighter Fresnel lens developed in France by Augustin-Jean Fresnel (pronounced fruh-nel). By 1858, all lighthouses in the first lighthouse district were using the Fresnel lens.

Architects created the plans for building or reconstructing lighthouses and keepers' dwellings, and engineers oversaw construction, only hiring qualified individuals to do the work, and higher quality materials were used, including bricks. The use of cast iron in Maine lighthouse construction began in the 1870s, and the cast iron towers were often lined with brick. The Board also established a routine system of inspections of lighthouses by qualified engineers rather than journeymen.

INSPECTORS

Inspectors would usually come around once or twice each year to inspect every lighthouse station. They were typically retired navy commanders with very high standards. At Great Duck Island Light, Dalton Reed, son of keeper Nathan Adam "Ad" Reed (1902-1912) recalled:

"They would wear white gloves. They would wipe their hands on the white walls to see if there was any dirt. Everything in the whistle house had to be polished for inspection because it was all brass. They would also come in and check out our house to see if it was neat and clean."

Inspectors were an important link between lightkeepers and the Lighthouse Establishment. They would report not only about the status of the upkeep of the light station but also the condition of the structures on the property. They would report storm damage and when repairs were needed, although, as you will see, despite some stations being in very deteriorated states, these repairs would often not happen for many years, sometimes upwards of ten or more. If a keeper wasn't doing his or her job and the station was unkempt and dirty, inspectors would recommend the removal of the keeper, which often happened much sooner than repairs. Keepers were typically removed within a year upon the recommendation of an inspector.

Inspector I.W.P. Lewis

One of the most frequently mentioned inspectors in this book is I.W.P. Lewis, nephew of Winslow Lewis. Born in 1808 in Charlestown, Massachusetts, Isaiah William Penn Lewis was a civil engineer and former master mariner who worked as a lighthouse designer, builder, engineer, and inspector. It is unclear when he began working for the Lighthouse Establishment, although his letter written in 1842 indicates that he was a part of the establishment since at least 1839.

I.W.P. Lewis was known as one of the most critical lighthouse inspectors, who held nothing back when writing his assessments of the condition of lighthouse stations or the lightkeepers in charge of them. Many letters were often written in response to his reports by lightkeepers at the stations he inspected refuting Lewis' claims of the deteriorated state of lighthouse stations. Lewis certainly wasn't out to win the popular vote and took his roles as engineer and inspector very seriously. Isaiah William Penn Lewis died on October 17, 1855, at the age of 47.

THE U.S. BUREAU OF LIGHTHOUSES (LIGHTHOUSE SERVICE)

In 1910, the United States again decided to reconfigure the lighthouse service and established the U.S. Bureau of Lighthouses. George R. Putnam, an engineer with the Coast and Geodetic Survey, was appointed Commissioner of Lighthouses and worked to remove political influence from the appointment of keepers, basing them solely on skill and merit. Putnam had a small staff and replaced the government-appointed military officer inspectors and engineers with civilians under the new title of "superintendent." He also worked to bring updated technology to lighthouses, like electricity and phones, to make keepers' work easier, and to improve the navigational aids. Putnam remained Commissioner of Lighthouses for 25 years until 1935, nearly the entire span of the Bureau of Lighthouses. At the end of his service, the United States had earned the second-safest shipping record in the world, with the Netherlands being the safest.

George Putnam, n.d., USLHS.

The U.S. Coast Guard

In 1939, the U.S. celebrated the 150th anniversary of the first federal lighthouse organization, the Lighthouse Establishment, and that same year, all active aids to navigation under the Lighthouse Service were transferred to the U.S. Coast Guard. Civilian lightkeepers were slowly phased out of manning light stations or joined the Coast Guard to continue their career in the lighthouse service. By 1990, the Coast Guard had automated every lighthouse in the United States, making it unnecessary for lighthouse keepers to live at the stations. The only exception is the Boston Harbor Island Lighthouse, established in 1716, which is the longest continually operating lighthouse in the United States and is still staffed today to commemorate the many men and women who tended the nation's lighthouses throughout history. The Coast Guard continues to update and maintain all active aids to navigation to this day.

The Maine Lights Program

After Maine's lighthouses were automated, the Coast Guard deemed many light station properties as excess and began to offer the properties for free to interested nonprofit parties to take over the maintenance and care of the structures at the stations. Many of the stations had fallen badly into disrepair after Coast Guardsmen left and required large sums of money to get the stations' structures back into working order. Some were too expensive, and if no organization stepped forward to take on the responsibilities, they were sold to private individuals.

Peter Ralston, who worked for the nonprofit Island Institute in Rockland, came up with the idea of the Maine Lights Program in 1993 while working with the Coast Guard to transfer the ownership of Heron Neck Lighthouse to the Island Institute. The drafted legislature sought to transfer 36 Maine lighthouses at no cost to nonprofit organizations to ensure the upkeep of the properties and guarantee public access, with the transfer of all 36 stations to be completed within a two-year time frame by 1998. Under the Maine Lights Program, the Coast Guard continues to maintain the aids to navigation within each structure, and the individual organizations are responsible for the upkeep of the lighthouse and all structures on the property. The legislature was signed on October 16, 1996, and the 36 properties were distributed among the United States Fish and Wildlife Agency, state agencies, municipalities, and many nonprofit organizations.

The National Historic Lighthouse Preservation Act (NHLPA)

The National Historic Lighthouse Preservation Act, signed in 2000, was modeled after the Maine Lights Program. The NHLPA works to transfer at no-cost light stations to federal agencies, local governments, nonprofit organizations, and educational and community development organizations. The goal is to preserve the cultural, recreational, and educational values associated with the nation's historic light stations.

Maine Open Lighthouse Day

Every September approximately 16 lighthouse stations along the coast of Maine open their doors to the public, offering a rare opportunity to learn about their history and heritage. Visitors can explore former keeper's homes, which are often set up as museums, and at some locations, you can climb the lighthouse tower. Stations that typically participate in the event are noted in the Contents section after the date the station was first established.

The event is sponsored by the United States Coast Guard, the Maine Office of Tourism, and the American Lighthouse Foundation. For more information visit the American Lighthouse Foundation website at **lighthousefoundation.org**.

MAINE LIGHTHOUSE RECORDS & INTERESTING FACTS

- Tallest lighthouse tower in New England- Boone Island Light, 133 feet
- First (and probably the only) baby born in a lighthouse under Coast Guard control- Browns Head Light
- First twin lighthouses in Maine- Cape Elizabeth Lights
- Only person to ever receive a Gold Life Saving Medal & Congressional Medal of Honor- keeper Marcus Hanna, Cape Elizabeth Lights
- Only surviving pair of range lights in the state- Doubling Point Range Lights
- First river light built in Maine- Fort Point Light
- Only lighthouses in Maine featuring a square exterior and circular brick interior- Deer Island Thorofare Light and Fort Point Light
- The first mention of fog bells used at lighthouses in the United States was in 1820 when an appropriation was made "for placing a bell near the lighthouse on West Quoddy Head"- West Quoddy Head Light
- The first lighthouses in the United States to be regularly equipped with steam whistles, consisting of a boiler and an 8 or 10-inch locomotive-type whistle, sounding an 8-second blast every minute, being the most powerful type of fog signal at that time (1869)- West Quoddy Head Light and Cape Elizabeth Light
- Last traditional lighthouse built in Maine- Isle au Haut Light, 1907
- Longest period of service for a keeper at the same lighthouse in the United States- keeper Charles Clement Skinner, 45 years at Marshall Point Light
- Only remaining maritime signal station in the United States- Portland Observatory
- First lighthouse in Maine featuring colored optics (red & white)- Monhegan Island Light, 1824
- Highest focal point in Maine- Seguin Island Light, 186 feet above sea level
- Shortest lighthouse in Maine- Portland Breakwater Light (Bug Light), 19.5 feet tall
- Last lighthouse built in Maine- Whitlocks Mill Light, 1910
- Last lighthouse automated in Maine- Goat Island, 1990
- The first lighthouse to be completed by the U.S. Government after it went into operation (1789) under the Lighthouses Act, and the oldest lighthouse in Maine- Portland Head Light, 1791
- Maine's first lightkeeper- Captain Joseph Greenleaf, Portland Head Light, (1791 to 1795, died in service)
- The only lighthouse in New England erected by an architect and engineer (according to lighthouse inspector I.W.P. Lewis)- Saddleback Ledge Light, 1839
- Only operational first-order Fresnel lens north of Rhode Island- Seguin Island Light
- Highest lighthouse above sea level in Maine- Seguin Island Light (focal plane 180 feet)
- The only caisson (sparkplug) style lighthouse accessible from land in the United States- Spring Point Ledge Lighthouse
- Last civilian lighthouse keeper in Maine after the Coast Guard assumed responsibility for the nation's lighthouses- Clarence Skolfield, 1968, Squirrel Point Light
- United States lighthouse that logged the most fog signal hours in 1885- West Quoddy Head Light, 1,945 hours
- Easternmost mainland point and easternmost lighthouse in the United States- West Quoddy Head Light
- Largest family to ever live at a lighthouse in the United States- Nathan Adams Reed, his wife, and their 17 children, Great Duck Island Light and Nash Island Light, 1902 to 1912 (died in service)
- Scene of the first naval battle of the American Revolution- Libby Island Light

Lighthouse Anatomy

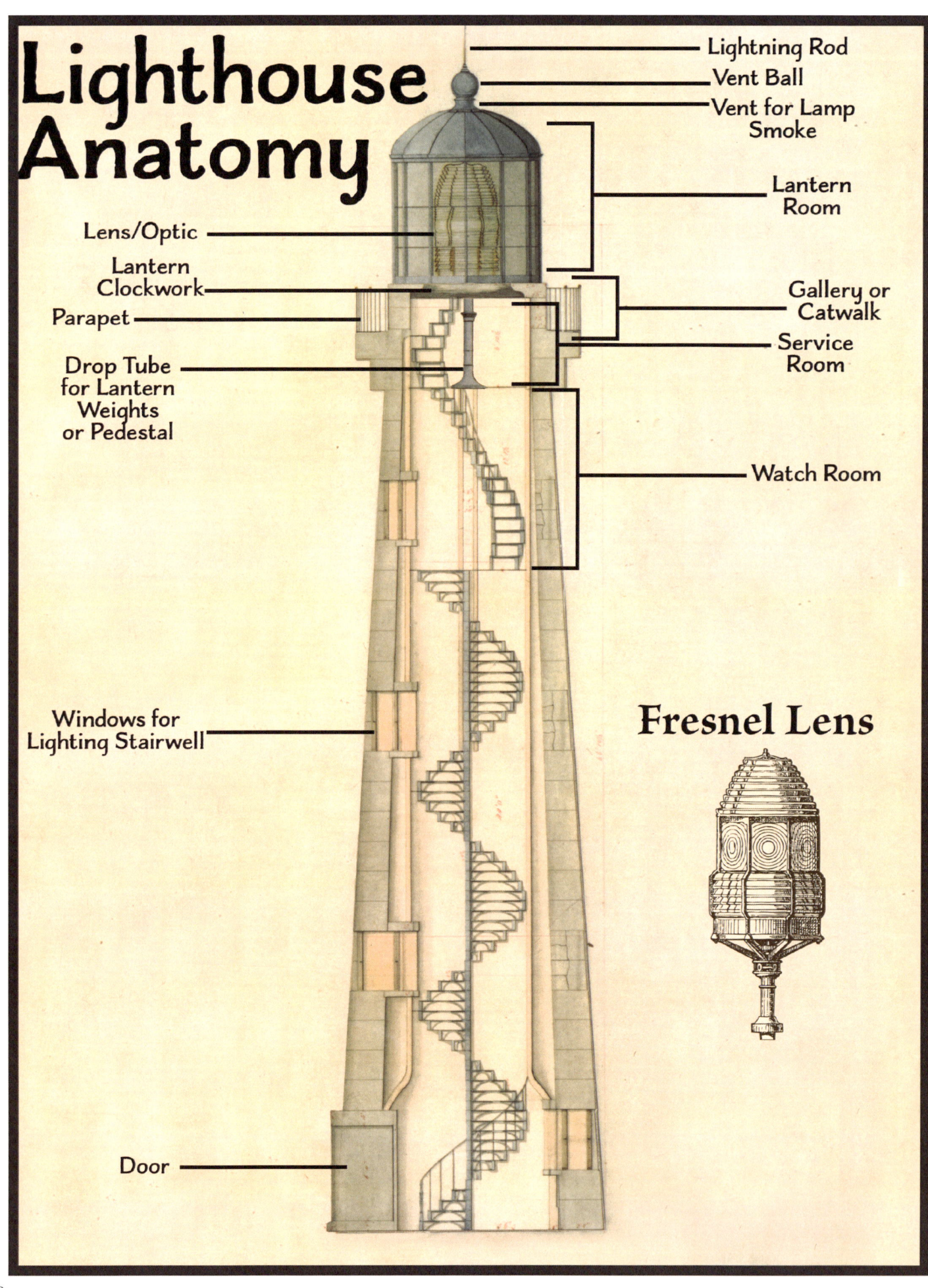

Lightning Rod

Vent Ball

Vent for Lamp Smoke

Lantern Room

Lens/Optic

Lantern Clockwork

Parapet

Gallery or Catwalk

Service Room

Drop Tube for Lantern Weights or Pedestal

Watch Room

Windows for Lighting Stairwell

Fresnel Lens

Door

LIGHTHOUSE-RELATED DEFINITIONS

Aerobeacon- A light assembly similar in looks to a spotlight, mounted on a base that rotates vertically by an electric motor. Aerobeacons are used to send fixed or flashing signals over long distances. They were popular due to their affordability and were easier to maintain than Fresnel lenses.

Bark, barque, or barc- A ship that has three or more masts and mainmasts rigged square, and only the mizzen (aftmost mast) rigged with fore and aft sails. They could operate with less crew than full-rigged ships and were considered workhorses in the mid-19th century.

Bosun's chair- Similar to a baby swing, it's is a chair, usually made of rope, that has two holes for your legs to dangle through, and surrounds your lower torso. It is attached to a rope or crane in order to help people get on land from a boat in difficult landing locations, or vice-versa.

Cistern- A brick structure usually kept in a basement to hold fresh water, which is typically collected from rain runoff from the roof. Many stations like island lighthouses did not have wells and had to rely on rain collected in the cisterns for all of their water.

Davit- A small crane used to hoist boats, equipment, supplies, and sometimes people!

Derrick (landing derrick)- Similar to a davit but larger, this is a tall post with a long boom arm that works like a large crane to lift heavy objects like boats, supplies, and again people in the case of lighthouse history.

Donkey Engine- A small steam-powered engine used to power a winch to hoist lighthouse boats up from the shore into the boathouse.

Fresnel lens- Pronounced "frey-nel," a composite, compact lens for lighthouses developed by French physicist Augustin-Jean Fresnel. It has a large aperture (opening) and short focal length and is lightweight. It has been known as "the invention that saved a million ships." Fresnel lenses became the choice lens to be installed in Maine lighthouses beginning around 1852, replacing the outdated lamps and reflectors.

Gaff- A long stick with a hook at the end used to grab objects from the ocean like buoy lines.

Isophase- A rhythmic lens light pattern of light followed by darkness. Example: "isophase 6 seconds" means six seconds of white light followed by six seconds of darkness.

Occulting light- A rhythmic lens light pattern where there are longer periods of light than darkness.

Oilbutts (oil-butts)- Tin or galvanized sheet iron cans used for holding oil for the light. Lightkeepers typically used 5-gallon (sometimes 3-gallon) oil cans to carry oil from the oil house to the top of the lighthouse to fuel the light. This was no easy feat at the tall lighthouses like Boon Island Light, which stood 133 feet tall!

Peapod- A small, double-ended boat, similar to a skiff or a dory, that is symmetrical from stern to stern. They were developed in Maine for lobstering around 1870 and were originally called "double-enders." The boat has a shallow draft making it possible to easily navigate rocky coastal Maine waters where large boats couldn't go. It was also easy to maneuver, which is why peapods were used by many lighthouse keepers.

Pinky- A small work boat primarily used for inshore fishing such as lobstering and gill-netting. They were usually operated by two people and could be sailed or rowed.

Range Lights- Two lighthouses at a single station that, when lined up, guided mariners to a safe channel leading into the harbor.

Sluiceway- An artificial channel water is let into through a sliding gate often used to carry away overflow water.

WHALEBACK LIGHT

Other Names: Whaleback Ledge Light, Whalesback Light, Whale's Back Light
Location: Whaleback Reef, Portsmouth Harbor, Piscataqua River, Kittery
Tower Height: 65 feet
Focal Plane Height: 68 feet
Year Built: 1830, 1872
First Lit: September 16, 1830, 1872
Fog Signal: Fog bell, horn, 2 blasts every 30 seconds
Past Optics: Two sets of lamps and reflectors, one ten feet above the other (1830), fourth-order Fresnel lens (1855), VRB-25 (2002)
Present Optic: VLB-44 (2009)
Range: 14 nautical miles
Characteristics: Two white flashes every 10 seconds
Year Automated: 1963
Year Deactivated: n/a
Status: Active aid to navigation
Keepers:
Head: Samuel E. Hascall, also spelled *Haskell* (1830 – 1839), Joseph L. Locke (1839 – 1840), Zachariah Chickering (1840), John Kennard (1840), Joseph B. Currier (1841), Eliphalet Grover (1841 – 1843), Joseph Prentiss Locke (1843 – 1847), Richard R. Locke (1847 – 1849), Jedediah Rand (1849 – 1853), Reuben T. Leavitt (1853 – 1859), Oliver N. Tucker (1859 – 1860), Gustavus A. Abbot (1860 – 1861), Joel P. Reynolds (1861 – 1864), Nathaniel P. Campbell (1864), Ambrose Card (1864), Gilbert D. Amee (1864 – 1869), James W. Varney (1869 – 1871), Augustus Ferdinand Barr (1871, died in service), William H. Caswell (1871 – 1872), Chandler Martin (1872 – 1878), Leander White (1878 – 1887), Ellison C. White (1887 – 1888), James M. Haley (1888 – 1893), Walter S. Amee (1893 – 1921), Arnold B. White (1921 – 1941).

First Assistant: Edward Parks (1863 – 1864), Ambrose Card (1864), Gilbert D. Amee (1864), **Mary M. Amee (1864 – 1867, died in service)**, Isaac W. Chauncy (1867 – 1868), Augustus F. Barr (1868 – 1871), Frederick Barr (1871), Frank P. Caswell (1871 – 1872), George B. Frost (1872 – 1873), Frank L. Chauncey (1873 – 1874), John Q.A. Martin (1874 – 1876), Frank L. Chauncey (1876 – 1880), John W. Lewis (1880 – 1882, died in service), Brackett Lewis (1882 – 1885), Ellison C. White (1885 – 1887), Daniel Stevens (1887 – 1890), John W. Robinson (1890 – 1893), James Haley (1893 – 1894), Wallace S. Chase (1894 – 1896), Alvah J. Tobey (1896 – 1899), John W. Wetzel (1899 – 1924, died in service), Maynard F. Farnsworth (1924 – 1941).

First Whaleback Lighthouse, c. 1859, USCGHO.

WHALEBACK LIGHT

11

Second Assistant: Emily F. Barr (1869 – 1871), James Haley (1892 – 1893), Wallace S. Chase (1893 – 1894), Alvah J. Tobey (1894 – 1896), Joseph A. Pruett (1896 – 1897), John W. Wetzel (1897 – 1899), John P. Brooks (1899 – 1915), James H. Schoppe (1915), Luther O. Poland (1915 – 1921), Maynard F. Farnsworth (1921 – 1924), Warren A. Alley (1925 – 1941).

Coast Guard Keepers: Maynard F. Farnsworth (1941 – 1944), Warren A. Alley (1941 – 1943), Everett W. Quinn (1947 – 1949), Morgan Willis (c. 1948-), Henry S. Brown (1955 – 1956), Robert Bedard (1955 – 1956), Arthur J. "Smiley" Smullen (1956), Clifford D. Evans (1956), Francis D. Hickey (1956 – 1957), Stephen H. Rogers (1956 – 1958), George E. Bee (c. 1957-), George A. Matheson (1958), Robert Brann (1959), Donald M. McDaniels (c. 1959-), Frank L. Loud (c. 1959 – c. 1960), Gerard J.R. Lambert (c. 1959 – 1960), James R. Pope (1959 – 1962), J.C. Yates (1960 – 1961), John C. Murphy (– 1960), George F. Johns (1960 – 1961), Allan L. Petersen (1961), Donald C. Gedney (1961), Wendell H. Griffin (1961), William J. Beasley (1961 – 1963), Roger C. Phillips (1961 – 1963), Charles E. Maddy (1962 – 1963), W.B. Collins (1962 – 1963), John Frasier (1963).

Second Whaleback Lighthouse, n.d.,
Penobscot Marine Museum Collection.

Visit: This lighthouse is best viewed by air or water. A distant view can be seen from Fort Foster Park in Kittery, on Pocahontas Road. Isles of Shoals Steamship Company and Portsmouth Harbor Cruises out of Portsmouth, New Hampshire, both offer cruises past the lighthouse.

HISTORY

Whaleback Ledge is one of the most difficult of all Maine's lighthouses I've written about. It isn't easy to find accurate, consistent information, in part due to the location- off the coast of New Hampshire yet in Maine waters, and when it was built, Maine had recently seceded from Massachusetts (1820), and some aspects of Maine's new government were still handled in Massachusetts. Whaleback Ledge is often referred to as belonging to New Hampshire in older articles and reports, and it is unclear when the ledge officially became part of Maine.

The first lighthouse constructed on Whaleback Ledge went to bid in 1829, at a time when Congress was required to accept the lowest bid despite the contractors' abilities and experience. The lowest bid came in at $20,306, close to $662,000 in today's dollars, and Daniel Haselton (often misspelled Hazelton) and William Palmer were the winning bidders.

Nearby Wood Island served as the location where tools and supplies were kept during construction. It was a slow process, as the ledge was less than an acre in size and only above water for a few hours each day at low tide. The circular granite base (referred to as a "pier") built on the ledge was 48 feet in diameter at the bottom, tapered to 32 feet at the top, and stood 22 feet high. Holes were drilled into the granite blocks on the bottom, and matching holes were drilled into the ledge. The granite blocks and ledge were doweled together using copper dowels to prevent the stones from moving when hit by crashing waves.

The superintendent, who goes unnamed in historical inspection reports, diverted from the original plans, which called for the contractors to make the ledge perfectly flat where the lighthouse was to sit, and instead ordered the contractors to lay the granite stones on the uneven surface of the ledge and fill the crevices with small stones, which were easily washed out. A 32-foot high rubblestone lighthouse was built on top of the pier that was 22 feet in diameter at the base and 11 feet in diameter at the top. Because the tower stood in the ocean most of the time, keepers had to use a hoisting system called davits to raise their dory from the ocean to the top of the granite pier to enter the lighthouse.

This is where historical documents, reports, and information in books begin to conflict with one another. Construction of the tower was most likely completed in 1830. Many sources say it was completed in 1829 or 1831, although neither of these years seems likely since the first keeper, Samuel Hascall (often misspelled Haskell), was appointed to the station in 1830. Keepers weren't typically appointed to a station before it was completed, nor would a station sit empty long after it was completed.

The lighthouse had a cellar, an external wooden storage shed attached to the outside of the lighthouse, and four rooms above the cellar to house the keepers divided into two levels. Lamps and reflectors were placed in the lantern room at the top, and to differentiate the lighthouse from nearby lighthouses, it showed two fixed white lights spaced apart by 10 feet vertically. In 1831, the entire lighthouse had to be cased over with a wooden "jacket" to prevent keeper Hascall "from being drowned out by the sea washing through all the crevices." This addition to the lighthouse is most likely why some sources state the lighthouse was completed in 1831. In 1837, the ocean side of the lighthouse received an additional casing of wooden sheathing "for the comfort and health of the keeper."

Whaleback Light was indeed poorly built, despite the bid being several times higher than other similar lighthouses built on submerged ocean ledges during that time. Much of the blame in articles and historical documents falls on the contractors, Haselton and Palmer. However, an unnamed "very honorable person," as inspector I.W.P. Lewis called him, was appointed the role of superintendent who oversaw, managed, and approved the lighthouse construction project.

In 1837, a breakwater pier was recommended to divert powerful ocean waves during storms from causing further damage to the exposed structure. Congress appropriated $20,000 from 1837 to 1838 for the project. In 1838, Stephen Pleasonton, Secretary of Treasury, contacted Colonel Sylvanus Thayer, founder of United States Military Academy at West Point, and renowned civil engineer and architect Alexander Parris from Boston, to

inspect the site and provide him with their assessment of the structure before the breakwater was built. They reported to Pleasonton that "no breakwater could secure the present building" and recommended a new lighthouse be built. In December 1838, Pleasonton submitted the recommendation to Congress with building plans for the new lighthouse drafted by Parris, which fell on deaf ears.

Keepers stated that during storms, the lighthouse felt like it was rocking like a cradle, and the ocean was so loud that the keepers could not hear each other speak over the sound of the waves crashing into the side of the lighthouse. It is also important to note that this station was a family station in the early years, with the head keeper's family living in the inferior structure and

Whaleback Light real photo postcard, n.d.,
Jeremy D'Entremont Collection.

WHALEBACK LIGHT

weathering violent storms together. It is unclear when the station became a stag station and their families lived on shore, but it most likely happened between the 1860s to 1890s when assistant keepers were appointed to the station, with the limited living space.

I.W.P. Lewis inspected Whaleback Light again in 1842. In his report, he states that the lighthouse was *"constructed of solid masonry, or intended to be, and yet so fraudulently done (although supervised by some very honorable person, whose name is suppressed from motives of delicacy)"* and that every year since it was built repairs had to be made. During his visit, workers were strapping the granite foundation blocks together with heavy iron bands. He went on to state, *"No human art can, however, make a firm structure of it. When there is a heavy swell rolling in, the base of the tower is struck with such force as to shake the whole edifice in the most alarming manner. The keeper asserted that the vibration was so great as to move the chairs and tables about the floor."*

By 1845, the lighthouse displayed two lights, one above the other spaced eight feet apart, and it was said that they looked like a single light at a distance of six miles away. In 1847, Congress appropriated an additional $25,000 to repair the granite pier and

Whaleback Light, notice the person suspended in the basket on the side of the lighthouse, n.d., USCGHO.

lighthouse and build a seawall out of riprap stone to further protect the structure from violent waves. In 1855, the lighthouse received a new fourth-order Fresnel lens, and in 1859, the station received a fog bell. In 1863, a fog bell with machinery was constructed at the station, which began operation on August 1.

In March 1868, a particularly violent storm created deep cracks in the lighthouse and foundation, broke all of the iron support bands around the granite pier, and dislodged stones from the upper section of the pier. Temporary repairs were made following the storm, and an urgent appeal was made to Congress to rebuild the lighthouse. Congress finally agreed the original lighthouse was in disrepair. On July 15, 1870, $70,000 was appropriated to build a new lighthouse on the ledge, not far from where the original one stood.

Work on the second lighthouse was also slow, as construction had to revolve around the tides. By the middle of 1871, the base, which was constructed of large granite blocks that were dovetailed together for stability, reached 20 feet above the low-water mark. In 1872, the new 65-foot lighthouse was completed, and the tower was fitted with a fourth-order Fresnel lens. In 1877, the old lighthouse tower temporarily housed the fog signal, although getting to the building was difficult in foul weather. By 1878, the cast-iron fog signal building was completed and fitted with a third-class Daboll trumpet operated by two steam engines. The old lighthouse was torn down in 1880.

In 1888, there were two third-class Daboll trumpets at the station, which were in operation for around 974 hours and consumed 16,895 pounds of coal. That same year, a fierce March storm tore away at the base of the original tower, which served to protect both the new lighthouse and fog signal building. A 20-foot high bulkhead was constructed of heavy pine timbers, and planking was bolted to both towers and to the ledge. The masonry from the demolished base of the original tower was dumped in the space between the bulkhead and towers to fill it in.

WHALEBACK LIGHT

Whaleback Light, n.d., USCGHO.

A second storm in 1888, this time in November, demolished more of the old base and washed away the landing derrick with its gear and rigging. Had the bulkhead not been built before this storm, it was believed the station would have been severely damaged or destroyed entirely. The washed-out stones were piled up on the ocean side of the tower to serve as a breakwater against the waves. That same year, a 70-foot boat slip that stretched from the ladder to the low-water line was constructed, and an iron gallery that spanned around the entire tower at the entryway level was added. A timber roof was built over the boat davits, and the fog signal received a new smoke stack.

In 1890, the station received a new traveling crane to hoist coal and other supplies up to the station, which was built in Boston. In 1898, a new fourth-order revolving lens was installed in the tower. In 1902, after complaints from several mariners that they saw the light station before hearing the fog signal, the old second-class Daboll trumpet was upgraded to a first-class Daboll trumpet. In 1912, the station received another new lens, a Barbier, Bernard, & Turenne Fresnel lens. This new lens had two valves and two bull's-eyes on both sides, which emitted a double flash every 10 seconds.

Early in 1963 Whaleback Light was automated, and the Coast Guard left the station. In 1969, the cast-iron fog signal tower was dismantled, and the base was demolished. In 1991, the intensity of the fog signal had to be reduced because the vibrations were damaging the lighthouse. The station was licensed to the American Lighthouse Foundation in October 2005, which joined forces with the town of Kittery to maintain the lighthouse. In November 2008, the station was given to the American Lighthouse Foundation at no cost from the Coast Guard. The foundation's local chapter, Friends of Portsmouth Harbor Lighthouse, continues to raise funds for the maintenance and restoration of the light.

STORIES
Who is John P. Decatur?

Remember when I.W.P. Lewis stated in his 1842 report that the construction of the lighthouse was *"supervised by some very honorable person, whose name is suppressed from motives of delicacy"* because this "honorable person" signed off on the poor construction of the lighthouse? That man was Colonel John Pine Decatur, who served in the War of 1812 in the Navy and died during his service as a Sutler in the Army.

Commodore Stephen Decatur, Jr.

Col. John P. Decatur was the brother of Commodore Stephen Decatur, Jr., who became a famous war hero for his efforts in the Barbary Wars and the War of 1812. Commodore Decatur had the first private residence in the White House neighborhood (Lafayette Square), built in 1819, known as the Decatur House. After only living there for 14 months after its completion, Commodore Decatur died at the home after an injury sustained in a duel against Commodore James Barron on March 22, 1820. The Decatur House is now a part of the White House Historical Association after being donated by the Beale family in 1956, who had lived there for over 80 years. Today, the Decatur House is a museum open to the public and houses a White House historical research center.

Election Scandal

But back to John Decatur. In 1821, Col. Decatur was the naval storekeeper at the Brooklyn Navy Yard. He and several other U.S. military officers used their high-ranking positions to try and thwart New York Governor DeWitt Clinton's reelection and install Daniel Tompkins, his opponent and sitting vice president at the time, in his place. Governor Clinton had proof of the attempts and presented them to the legislature. Col. Decatur and the others were implicated, and their superiors were informed of the scandal.

The Monroe administration was very displeased, especially since the vice president would have benefitted from the scandal, which looked bad for the administration if no action had been taken against Col. Decatur and the others. Secretary of the Navy Smith Thompson ordered Col. Decatur to be transferred to a smaller post in Portsmouth, New Hampshire in 1823, maintaining the same position he held in New York.

Col. Decatur and the President

Col. Decatur was so upset by the orders to be transferred that he personally went and visited President James Monroe about the letter he received from Thompson. In a letter from President Monroe to Thompson, dated August 27, 1823, he describes the encounter and explains that he told Col. Decatur that *"although dissatisfaction was felt at his conduct, no dishonorable motive was imputed to him."* Col. Decatur didn't stop there by trying to use his position for political influence. In 1824, he was implicated again, this time for influencing a New York Senate member to vote in favor of incorporating the controversial Chemical Bank, which, if passed, he would have earned personal gains from.

John P. Decatur, n.d., painted by Joseph Wood.

The Decatur Cannon

In September 1824, President Monroe invited Marquis de La Fayette, a French aristocrat and the only surviving general of the American Revolutionary War at that time, to come to the United States for a tour around the country with him to celebrate the 50th anniversary of the American Revolution. Col. Decatur accompanied the party, which eventually reached Caldwell, New Jersey. The local militia brought out an old cannon and fired it to commend the occasion, and the blast destroyed it. Col. Decatur was so impressed with the salute and enthusiasm of the militiamen that he presented the village with a replacement brass cannon that had belonged to his late brother, Commodore Decatur, to mark the occasion.

In 1816, Congress voted for the cannon and other trophies to be awarded to Commodore Decatur for his victories in the war with Algiers. The cannon was displayed in the park in the center of Caldwell, where it remained until the Civil War. The town was concerned it would end up in the hands of the Confederacy and, therefore, stored it temporarily in Trenton. After the war, it was returned to the park, where it remained until 1968 when it was stolen. The town of Caldwell continues to search for the missing Decatur Cannon, hoping it will one day be returned.

President Andrew Jackson

Despite his scandalous actions and implications, when Andrew Jackson became president on March 4, 1829, he appointed Col. Decatur the Collector of Customs in Portsmouth, New Hampshire, on April 8, just one month after gaining the presidency. Col. Decatur was a very close friend of Andrew Jackson, so much so that he named one of his children Andrew Jackson Decatur.

Another Scandal?

So, what does all of this have to do with a lighthouse in Maine? It ties in with the poor construction of Whaleback Light, which resulted in miserable, unsafe, and unfit conditions endured by early keepers and the eventual need to rebuild the structure entirely. A congressional report dated March 2, 1832, states that on May 12, 1829, "*Daniel Haselton and William Palmer entered into a contract with John P. Decatur...to construct the foundation, and erect a lighthouse, on the ledge of rocks called the Whale's Back.*" The report is regarding Haselton and Palmer seeking to get reimbursed by the government for the copper dowels they used to secure the granite foundation blocks of the lighthouse to the ledge instead of the stone dowels the plans called for, which they paid for out of pocket.

The report makes it very clear that Decatur is the superintendent of the construction project, which took place during his time serving as the Collector of Customs in Portsmouth. It also says that their contract states, "*the superintendent reserves the right to make such alterations as may, in progress of the work, be found necessary, either for security or convenience of the lighthouse.*" This means that Decatur had the power to alter the plans and order the contractors to make changes as he saw fit, including his admission that he ordered the men to use copper bolts and pay for them at their own expense. Decatur did not believe the contractors should be reimbursed for the extra expense, although a clause in the contract stated that if changes were ordered, they would be reimbursed.

In the End

It is unclear why Decatur did not want the contractors compensated for an extra expense that he ordered, but it is clear that he was in charge of the lighthouse's construction and signed off on its quality. The men were finally compensated in 1834, five years after construction on Whaleback Light began, for $778.25, the exact amount they spent on the copper bolts.

Whaleback Light aerial view, n.d., USCGHO.

Col. John Decatur moved on to become Sutler in the Army at Fort Gibson in Oklahoma in April 1831 and died November 12, 1832, from typhoid fever, just two years after the lighthouse was completed. When I.W.P. Lewis wrote his report regarding the history and condition of Whaleback Light, intentionally leaving out the name of the superintendent of the project, Decatur had been deceased for ten years. Despite his apparent shady dealings and poor judgment on lighthouse construction, he was clearly well respected by many, even after his death.

Daniel Haselton built the Middle Street Baptist Church in Portsmouth, NH, in 1826. He and William Palmer also built the custom house in Newburyport, Massachusetts, in 1835, which is now a museum. Haselton then built the first lighthouse on Robbins Reef in New Jersey in 1839, which stood for 44 years before being replaced by a steel lighthouse. In reports from inspectors, the Robbins Reef lighthouse received great reviews and needed little repair throughout the years. And so the question remains: Was the poor construction of the lighthouse Decatur's fault, the contractors' fault, or all of the above? We may never know.

WHALEBACK LIGHT

Not a Desirable Post

After serving nine years at Whaleback Light, the first keeper, Samuel E. Hascall, submitted his resignation on September 19, 1839, as the lighthouse had continued to deteriorate and become less stable with every passing year. John L. Locke was appointed a temporary keeper at the station, and Portsmouth, New Hampshire's Collector of Customs House, Superintendent of Lights Daniel Drown wrote, *"Under these circumstances, unless the new Keeper, Mr. Locke, is perfectly willing to encounter the risk, I would respectfully recommend that the Light be discontinued until a new building can be erected."* Secretary of Treasury Pleasonton felt the lighthouse was necessary for the safety of mariners and worth the structural risk and decided to keep it in operation. In response, Drown requested that the keeper have the option to abandon the station "whenever a storm shall render it dangerous for him to remain."

Locke, currently keeper at White Island Light, accepted the risk and was to report to the station on October 1. A week later, eager to leave the station, keeper Hascall contacted Superintendent Drown and told him that Locke had failed to show up to replace him. The following day, Drown appointed Zachariah Chickering temporary keeper at the station. Upon Chickering's arrival at the light, he discovered Locke had just shown up and had to turn around and return to the mainland, receiving $1.64 in pay for his efforts.

Toward the end of the month, Drown came out to the lighthouse and found that Lock was gone and had appointed someone else to take care of the light. Drown found Locke and ordered him back to his post, but only a few weeks later, he discovered that Locke had only stayed at the lighthouse two nights since he had left. Drown discharged Locke from the position and appointed Chickering in his place.

Unforgiving Seas

Despite how close Whaleback Light is to the mainland compared to other stations, the waves were still unforgiving and violently tore at the structures in winter storms. One storm in 1886 broke a window in the lighthouse and nearly drowned the keepers as the water rushed in. Head keeper Leander White flew a white sheet from the top of the tower in hopes that someone would see his distress signal and send help, but the wind and the waves were too violent, and it was torn apart. After the storm, the hole from the broken window was fitted with a granite block.

A Highly Desirable Station

The station became much more desirable after the new lighthouse was built in 1872. It wasn't very far from the mainland or the city of Portsmouth, New Hampshire. Keeper Walter S. Amee was head keeper from 1893 to 1921, a total of 28 years. It is said that, at that time, his two co-workers held the record of the longest-serving keeper assistants in the district (and may still be). John Wetzel was at Whaleback from 1897 to 1899 as second assistant keeper, then he was promoted to first assistant keeper, which he served from 1899 to 1924, a total of 27 years. Second assistant keeper John P. Brooks came to the station when Wetzel was promoted and served at the station with Amee and Wetzel from 1899 to 1915, a total of 16 years. Both assistant keepers had been offered promotions at other stations but turned them down to stay on Whaleback.

Whaleback Light aerial view after 1969, n.d., USCGHO.

WHALEBACK LIGHT

Before coming to Whaleback Light, Walter Amee had been a sailor. He left his position aboard the schooner *Eldorado* out of Kittery Point in the summer of 1873. The vessel sailed toward the Grand Banks that summer, and the ship and seven crew members were never seen or heard from again. That information didn't deter Amee from a life at sea. He captained two separate fishing schooners soon after until he was appointed as second assistant keeper at the Boon Island Light station in 1891. He spent two years there before being transferred and promoted to first assistant keeper at Isle of Shoals. He was only there for seven months before he was again transferred and promoted to head keeper at Whaleback Light. Amee's assistants never had the chance to get promoted at Whaleback since, after he left, Arnold B. White, transferred from Little Harbor Breakwater in Massachusetts, took over as head keeper in 1921 and remained there until 1941.

Deaths in Service

Agustus Ferdinand Barr

Civil War veteran Augustus Ferdinand Barr was promoted from first assistant keeper to head keeper in March 1871. Only three months later, Barr was tending his lobster traps while his wife was away in the city, leaving their three children alone at the lighthouse. The children watched as Barr's boat capsized in the heavy seas, tossing him into the waves. They sent out a distress signal which a watchman at the nearby Wood Island Hospital (Wood Island Life Saving Station) saw. Two men attempted to rescue Barr, heading out to where he had last been seen. The swell of the huge seas had been too great, and Barr had drowned; his body was never found.

John Lewis

For a period of time, the fog signal tower was painted red. It was a dangerous job, given that the keepers had to be suspended from the top of the building, and in late June of 1882, the first assistant keeper, John W. Lewis, had to paint the building. He was painting the very top of the foghorn pipe when he fell to the rocks below. Although he was transported to shore for medical attention, he later died from his injuries.

Mary Amee and John Wetzel

Deaths due to underlying medical conditions or diseases were not uncommon in the earlier years of lighthouse history. Mary M. Amee, one of two females who held lighthouse keeper positions at Whaleback Light, passed

away while on leave from the lighthouse due to illness and died in 1867 from tuberculosis at the age of 32. In December 1924, John W. Wetzel was also on leave from his post, expecting to return in just a few days, and passed away unexpectedly at his home at the age of 57 from a cerebral hemorrhage.

Flying Santa Mishap

Historian and pilot Edward Rowe Snow was the "Flying Santa" for New England lighthouse families for 40 years. Every year at Christmastime, Snow would get in his airplane and airdrop packages filled with gifts to lighthouse stations. One year, he missed the mark at Whaleback with his first attempt, and the package landed in the sea. He circled back around and was successful with his second attempt. It wasn't until weeks later that someone found the package that was lost at sea, almost 90 miles away in Cape Cod! ⚓

WHALEBACK LIGHT

CAPE NEDDICK LIGHT

Other Names: Nubble Light, The Nubble, Cape Neck
Location: York
Tower Height: 41 feet
Focal Plane Height: 88 feet
Year Built: 1879
First Lit: July 1, 1879
Fog Signal: Bell on lighthouse (1879), framework bell tower and striking mechanism (1880), 2,035-pound bell with striking apparatus (1890), pyramidal bell tower and 3,000-pound bell (1911), diaphragm horn (1969), currently horn, 1 blast every 10 seconds
Past Optics: Fourth-order Fresnel lens (1879)
Present Optic: Fourth-order Fresnel lens (1928)
Range: 13 nautical miles
Characteristics: Isophase red 5 seconds
Year Automated: 1987
Year Deactivated: n/a
Status: Active aid to navigation
Keepers: Leander White (1879- reassigned before the lighthouse was established), Simon Leighton (1879- resigned due to illness before the lighthouse was established), Nathaniel H. Otterson (1879 – 1885), Brackett Lewis (1885 – 1904), William M. Brooks (1904 – 1912), James M. Burke (1912 – 1919), William P. Richardson (1919 – 1921), Fairfield H. Moore (1921 – 1928), Edmund A. Howe (1928 – 1930), Truman M. Lathrop (1930), Eugene L. Coleman (1930 – 1943).

Coast Guard Keepers: Warren A. Alley (1943 –), Oscar M. Sparrow (1940s), Wilbur I. Brewster (1948 – 1951), Irving T. Sparrow (1951 – 1953), Robert McWillimas (1954 – 1956), Bruce C. Reed (1957 – 1959), Boyd J. Davis (1961), John Johnson (1960s), Arnold P. Chadwick (1960s), John H. Johnson (1961-1962), George P. Pistey (1962-1963), Leo R. Midgett (1963-1965), Wilson E. Allen (1965-1966), David K. Winchester (1966-1967), John P. Reidy (1966-1967), Alfred Paul Chadwick (1967 – 1969), Lindsay N. Rome (1969-1970), Daniel J. Fries (1970-), Michael Carbino (c. 1971 – 1973), Michael Hackett (1973 – 1975), Richard Harrison (1975 – 1977), Ronald O'Brien (1977 – 1979), John Terry (1979 – 1984), Robert French (1984 – 1986), Russell Ahlgren (1986 – 1987).

Visit: The lighthouse and grounds are not open to the public, but Sohier Park in York Beach offers excellent views of the lighthouse.

CAPE NEDDICK LIGHT

HISTORY

The 1842 wreck of the *Isidore* prompted the need for a lighthouse at Cape Neddick. In 1852, $5,000 was appropriated to build the lighthouse, but it was then withdrawn when a survey of the coast deemed it unnecessary. The Lighthouse Board petitioned for the lighthouse to be built again in 1874, which was approved, but construction was delayed until February 1879 due to difficulties in purchasing the property from multiple property owners.

The cast-iron sections of the lighthouse were built in Portland and transported aboard the *USS Myrtle* in April 1879. The interior was lined with red brick, and a thirty-two-step cast-iron spiral staircase led to the top. One of the most unique features of Cape Neddick Light is the miniature lighthouse finials, decorative replicas of the lighthouse itself, that line the gallery railing (see top photo on previous page).

The Victorian "gingerbread style" keeper's house had six rooms in total. It had a large parlor stove for heat, a kitchen and pantry, a living room, a dining room, and three bedrooms upstairs.

The tower was originally painted white, shortly after, it was changed to a reddish brown and then painted white again in 1899. In 1888, a boathouse and boat slip were built, and then in 1898, a telephone line was installed. In 1902, the oil house was added, and in 1928, an explosion damaged the Fresnel lens and another one was brought from another station.

The fog bell was originally suspended from an A-frame tower, and in 1890, a striking machine was added. In 1911, an enclosed pyramidal tower was built to house the bell, and it remained there until 1961.

The lighthouse was automated in 1987, which upset many of the townspeople. They, together with the Maine Lights Program, adopted the station in 1998. One of the biggest draws to Cape Neddick Light is the Lighting of the Nubble, a yearly festival of lights where the station's buildings are covered in Christmas lights beginning in late November.

Aerial photo of Cape Neddick Lighthouse, 1960, USCGHO.
CAPE NEDDICK LIGHT

STORIES

Booming Tourism Trade Side-Businesses

Cape Neddick Light has always been a popular draw among tourists, and on more than one occasion, lightkeepers and their families cashed in on that popularity. Today, it is estimated that half a million people visit Sohier Park every year to look at the lighthouse. It has become an American icon as a classic example of a lighthouse, so much so that a photograph of the lighthouse is included on the Voyager Gold Record on the *Voyager II* spacecraft alongside other prominent man-made structures like the Great Wall of China and Taj Mahal, meant to be viewed by intelligent extraterrestrials should they find it.

Keeper Nathaniel Otterson

In 1879, keeper Nathaniel Otterson and his family were the first of many to cash in on the tourism trade. They allowed visitors from 10 am-6 pm, and his son would row tourists over to the island for ten cents. Keeper Otterson's annual salary was $500, not including profits from his tourism business. His ability to use government property for a side business was probably ignored due to the fact that he was the cousin of New Hampshire Governor Natt Head.

Keeper Brackett Lewis

This practice continued for many years, and in 1898, keeper Brackett Lewis was told he could not admit visitors on Sundays, most likely because it interfered with his duties. He was so good at tuning out the station's fog bell that sometimes he forgot to deactivate it. The 3,000-pound bell could be heard six miles away by the keepers at Boon Island!

Keeper William M. Brooks

From 1904 to 1912, William M. Brooks was lightkeeper and also a successful tour operator. He offered lighthouse tours by his wife for 5 cents, and fishing tackle and bait as well. Their business was too successful, and he was fired when his superiors wrote there were "200-300 people at certain times to roam about the reservation with only the keeper's wife to care for the government property."

Keeper James Burke

Keeper James Burke succeeded Brooks in 1912. The family had a cow and chickens and harvested mussels, crabs, lobster, fish, and ducks from around their island home. Local lobstermen were known to toss a sack of lobsters on the island on their way back to the dock in appreciation for the family keeping them safe. Burke's daughter Lucy wrote that sometimes, at night, flocks of birds would crash into the tower, and hundreds of dead ones would have to be raked up in the morning. When keeper Burke retired in 1919, his successor, William Richardson, was fired for bringing tourists to the island.

Haunted Waters

Deadly Premonitions of the *Isidore*

Thirty-seven years before a lighthouse was to be built on Cape Neddick, a haunting, historical shipwreck occurred on its shores. The story of the *Isidore* has many different versions, right down to the spelling of the ship's name, often spelled *Isadore*, although every version includes deadly premonitions. The ship was docked in Kennebunkport, Maine, preparing for her maiden voyage to sail a load of lumber to New Orleans and then onward to France. It was scheduled to set sail on Wednesday, November 30, 1842.

On November 26, 1842, crewmember Thomas King had a dream. There are two versions of his dream: one is that he dreamt about the wreckage of a ship that looked like *Isidore*, with its crew washed up on the shore. The second version was that he dreamt he saw a long, wind-swept shore where there were seven crudely-built wooden coffins lined up on the beach. Although he saw no one, he called out, asking who the coffins were for, and "For the crew of *Isidore*" was the reply.

CAPE NEDDICK LIGHT

King went to Captain Leander Foss and told him about the dream and begged him to be left ashore. Capt. Foss dismissed King's premonition and told him he had to go because he had been paid in advance. Capt. Foss was known for being stubborn as a mule and had already wrecked two ships under his command. At one point, he proclaimed that should he lose another ship, he hoped his "head would be found under the mast."

George P. Davis, the 18-year-old cabin boy aboard the *Isidore*, had a dying sister, Roxana. She begged him not to go because she wouldn't survive long enough for his return. Oddly, he told her, "I shall be the one to go first." He left and walked to the building at the edge of the wharf and carved "George Parkins Davis" before setting sail. Roxana died the following month, on December 28.

Others who were to be aboard the ship had bad dreams and omens that week as well. Crewmember John Crowder heard dogs howling outside his home for three nights in a row. Captain Paul Grant, a passenger on the ship, also had a dream of seven coffins with his own body lying in one of them.

Thomas King was so afraid of his dream that he decided he was not going to go. The entire crew greatly feared the captain, and so he deserted under the cover of darkness and hid in the backcountry so as to not be found. The morning the *Isidore* was to set sail the captain noticed King was missing, but it was too late to find a replacement, and the ship sailed one crewmember short.

Ignore the Warnings and Sail On
On November 30, 1842, *Isidore* set sail at 10 am, despite warnings of foul weather coming. A crowd gathered in Kennebunkport, where many of the crew were from, to watch the *Isidore* depart. Many people in the crowd remarked how unusually red the western sky was. There wasn't much wind as the ship left the port, and it is claimed that a sudden snow squall passed through, and as the sun shined through the snow, it turned the sky the color of blood.

The ship had only sailed a few miles when a deadly Nor'easter moved in, dumping more than a foot of snow with high winds that turned the sea into a deathtrap. The ship could not stay on course, and no more than 12 hours after setting sail, the ship smashed into Bald Head Cliff, just north of where the lighthouse would be built 37 years later. The ship was torn to pieces, and not a soul survived the wreck.

The next day, wreckage from the ship began washing ashore. About a week later, seven bodies washed ashore, including Captain Leander Foss. One story claims that his leg washed ashore several days after his body, and yet another claims that Captain Foss' head was indeed found under a part of the mast that had washed ashore along with his body. Local legend has it that the *Isidore* and her phantom crew can be seen sailing past the Cape Neddick Light on stormy nights.

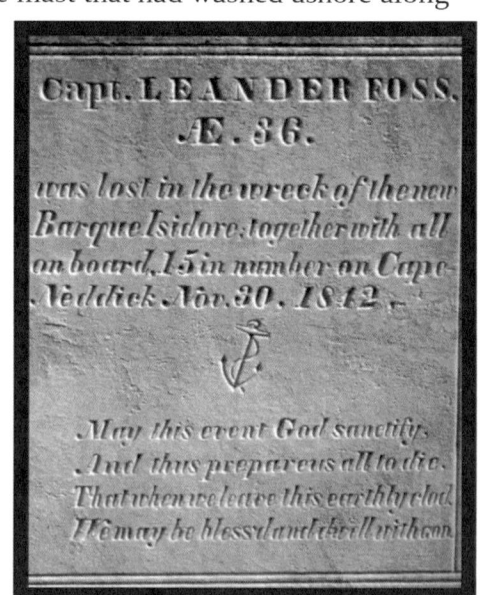

Isidore Crew
Bold names are those who washed ashore.
Leander Foss, 36, Captain, Village Cemetery, Kennebunkport
Clement P. Stone, 25, 1st Mate, Perkins Cemetery, Kennebunkport
John Crowder, 45, 2nd Mate, lost at sea
Capt. Paul M. Grant, 42, Passenger, lost at sea
George Parkins Davis, 18, Cabin Boy, Village Cemetery, Kennebunkport
George P. Lewis, 15, Seaman, Village Cemetery, Kennebunkport
John Tendell, 53, Cook, lost at sea
James C. Murphy, 23, Seaman, Village Cemetery, Kennebunkport
George F. Hutchins, 23, Seaman, lost at sea

CAPE NEDDICK LIGHT

Alvin Huff, 23, Seaman, lost at sea
William J. Thompson, 18, Seaman, Thompson Cemetery, Arundel
Daniel H. Perkins, 22, Seaman, Merrill Cemetery, Kennebunkport
James Young, 23, Seaman, lost at sea
Charles Lord, 25, Seaman, lost at sea
William B. Harding, 22, Seaman, lost at sea

Life at Cape Neddick Lighthouse

Lighthouse Cat

One of the most popular residents that lived at Cape Neddick Light was Sambo Tonkus or Mr. T., a beefy, 20-pound tomcat. The cat loved the lighthouse so much that his owner, keeper Truman Lathrop, left him at the station when he relocated.

Apparently, Mr. T. ate all the mice on the island and was hungry, so he decided to go find some more mice. Keeper Eugene Coleman reported that he was shocked when he saw the tomcat paddling to the mainland one day. Later on, Mr. T. returned with a big, fat mouse. The orange-striped cat became so popular among visitors that he got his own article in the newspapers, which heavily praised his incredible swimming ability.

Trolley Basket Baby

All of the supplies the lightkeepers needed had to be carried across the rocks, then placed in a large basket on the mainland that was suspended by a 200-yard wire that stretched across the water. They would then row over to the island and reel the basket over from the mainland.

In 1967, Coast Guard Keeper David Winchester found an unorthodox way to use the basket trolley. Winchester put his 7-year-old son Rickie in the basket and send the basket over the rocky ledges and 50 feet above the ocean to the mainland where someone would pick him up. It was faster than rowing!

When an Associated Press photographer snapped a photo of Rickie in the basket suspended above the waves, it got a lot of attention, so much so that Coast Guard superiors put a stop to the trolley basket baby fiasco and decided that no families with school-aged children could be stationed at the lighthouse ever again.

CAPE NEDDICK LIGHT

Boon Island Light Station, 1951, USCG.

BOON ISLAND LIGHT

BOON ISLAND LIGHT

Other Names: Boone Island Light
Location: Boon Island, York
Tower Height: 133 feet
Focal Plane Height: 137 feet
Year Built: 1799 unlit 50-foot wooden tower daybeacon, 1805 unlit 40-foot stone tower daybeacon, 1811 32-foot lighthouse, 1832 height of tower increased, 1852 to 1855 present 133-foot granite tower
First Lit: 1811, January 1, 1855
Fog Signal: Hand-rung bell on oil house roof (1890), currently automated fog horn, one blast every 10 seconds
Past Optics: Lamps and reflectors (1811), second-order Fresnel lens (1855)
Present Optic: Solar-powered VEGA VRB-25 (1993)
Characteristics: Flashing white light every 5 seconds
Range: 19 nautical miles
Year Automated: 1980
Year Deactivated: n/a
Status: Active aid to navigation, privately owned
Keepers:
Head: Benjamin Wane (1811), David Oliver (1811 – 1812), Thomas Hanna (1812 – 1816), Eliphalet Grover (1816 – 1839), Joseph P. Junkins (1839 – 1840), Mark Dennet (1840 – 1841), John S. Thompson (1841 – 1843), John Kennard (1843 – 1844), Isidore S. Thompson (1844), John Kennard (1844 – 1846), Nathaniel Baker (1846 – 1849), John S. Thompson (1849 – 1853), Hiram Tobey (1853), Caleb L. Goold (1853 – 1854), George Bowder (1854 – 1855), Josiah Tobey (1855 – 1859), Nathaniel Baker (1859), Joseph H. Hart (1859 – 1861), George B. Wallace (1861), Benjamin Bridges (1861 – 1864), R.C. Yeaton (1864 – 1867), Joshua K. Card (1867 – 1874), Alfred J. Leavitt (1874 – 1886), Orrin M. Lamprey (1886 – 1888), William C. Williams (1888 – 1911), Mitchell Blackwood (1911 – 1916), Harry Smith (1916 – 1920), Albert Staples (1920 – 1923), Harold I. Hutchins (1924 – 1933), Charles E. Tracy (1933 – 1937), Hoyt P. Smith (1937 – 1942).

First Assistant: Christopher C. Littlefield (1854), George G. Bowden (1854 – 1855), Charles H. Tobey (1855 – 1859), William Baker (1859), Josiah Tobey, Jr. (1859 – 1861), Calvin Gray (1861 – 1866), George H. Yeaton (1866 – 1867), John W. Card (1867 – 1873), Leander White (1874 – 1878), David R. Grogan (1878 – 1880), George O. Leavitt (1880 – 1881), Paschal Fernald (1881 – 1885), Orrin M. Lamprey (1885 – 1886), William C. Williams (1886 – 1888), James Burke (1888 – 1890), Charles W. Torry (1890 – 1893), William M. Brooks (1893 – 1897), Charles S. Williams (1897 – 1905), William T. Stevens (1905), Mitchell Blackwood (1905 – 1911), Charles W. Allen (1911 – 1913), Fuller E. Larrabee (1913), Roger P. Philbrick (1913 – 1917), Roscoe M. Chandler (1917 – 1919), Harry M. Kelley (1919 – c. 1921), Eugene L. Coleman (1924 – 1930), Frederick C. Batty (1930 – 1932), Charles E. Tracy (c. 1933), Benjamin Stockbridge (c. 1935), Hoyt P. Smith (1936 – 1937), Harry H. McClure (1937 – 1940), George A. McKenney (1940 – 1942).

Second Assistant: Samuel Tobey (1855 – 1856), Josiah Tobey Jr. (1856 – 1859), John S. Baker (1859), Enos Gray (1859 – 1861), S. Tobey (1861 – 1864), George E. Bridges (1864 – 1865), Charles Ramsdell (1865 – 1868), Samuel R. McLorn (1868), Luther Amazeen (1868 – 1870), Nathan White, Jr. (1870 – 1874), Edwin J. Hobbs (1874 – 1876), David R. Grogan (1876 – 1878), George O. Leavitt (1878 – 1880), Paschal Fernald (1880 – 1881), Orrin M. Lamprey (1881 – 1885), William C. Williams (1885 – 1886), James Burke (1886 – 1888), Leonidas H. Sawyer (1888 – 1890), Charles W. Torry (1890), Walter S. Amee (1891 – 1893), William M. Brooks

1893), Alvah J. Toby (1893 – 1894), James Hawe (1894), Joseph A. Pruett (1894 – 1896), Charles S. Williams 1896 – 1897), Meshach M. Seaward (1897 – 1900), Merton E. Tolman (1900), Henry C. Neal (1900 – 1902), Frank L. Peabbles (1902), Leroy L. Myers (1902), James R. Faulkingham (1902 – 1903), William T. Stevens 1903 – 1904), Mitchell Blackwood (1905), William Henry Burns (1905 – 1907), Charles Whitten Allen (1907 - 1911), Fuller E. Larrabee (1912 – 1913), Charles A. Radley (1913), Albert Staples (1914 – 1916), Roscoe M. Chandler (1916 – 1917), Harry M. Kelley (1917 – 1919), George E. Woodward (1919 – 1920), Arthur E. Ginn c. 1921), Eugene L. Coleman (1923 – 1924), Myron L. Wilson (1924 – 1925), Andrew H. Kennedy (1925 – 1928), Fred C. Batty (1930), Frank M. Rumery (c. 1930), Clinton L. "Buster" Dalzell (c. 1932), Howard R. Gray 1932 – 1934), Hoyt P. Smith (1935 – 1936), Harry H. McClure (1936 – 1937), Henry S. Brown (1937 – c.1941).

Coast Guard Keepers: Warren Alley (1941-1943), Charles U. Gardner (c. 1942-1943), Calvin Dolby (1944-1945), Jack McCoe (1944-1945), William Parmenter (1944-1945), John H. Morris (c. 1945), Thomas J. Guice c. 1945), Russell G. Carpenter (c. 1945), Archie McLaughlin (c. 1947), Clifford Gustavson (c. 1947), Robert Adams (c. 1947), Gordon B. Kenny (1951-1952), Charles Kendrick Capon (1951-1953), Jerry Russell (c. 1954), Harold L. Roberts (1956), Leonard John "Moon" Mullen (1958-1961), Robert Brann (c. 1958), Ron Schultz 1959), Albert B. Mize (c. 1960), Frank R. Goodwin (c. 1960), Paul K. Jordan (1960-1961), Earle D. Andrews 1960-1961), George V. Joy (1961), Thomas J. Dunwoodie (1961-1962), William R. Lockard (1961-1962), Philip R. Ghilders (1962), Charles Eaton (1962-1964), James W. Eyles (1962-1965), R.W. Kolb (1962-1965), Randall E. Lavigne (1963-1964), Carlos R. Earnest (1964-1965), Earl L. Williams (1965-1966), G.D. Sabbagh 1965-1966), Arnold H. Benard (1965-1966), Arthur D. Blackburn (1965-1967), Lawrence V. Jordan (1966-1967), David Wells (1966-1967), Lucien R. Tessier (1966-1967), Johnnie A. Raburn (1967), August "Gus" Pfister (1967-1968), Raymond Clark Jr. (July 1967 - July 1968), Donald W. Nield (1967-1968), Larry E. Miller 1968-1969), John J. Von Atzinger (1968-1969), Jack N. Walters (1968-1969), Leroy A. Brown (1968-1970), R.L. Ross (c. 1969), James E. Zielaskowski (c. 1969), D.E. Crawford (c. 1969), Robert Edwards (officer in charge, c. 1970-1973), Garth Clough (c. 1970-1972), Thomas J. Lee (July 1970 to October 1971), Bob Roberts 1971-1972), Richard Heon (early 1970s), Stephen Garsznksi (c. 1972), Fred Kendall (1973-1975), Jack W. Straley (Feb. 1977-Feb. 1978), William Ripka (c. 1977-1978), Kirby Eldridge (1978), Leo Berry (c. 1978).

Visit: Boon Island Lighthouse is best seen by boat or air, although a distant view can be seen from Cape Neddick Lighthouse and Long Sands Beach in York. New England Eco Adventures out of their Kennebunk location offers two different tours that pass by Boon Island.

HISTORY

Boon Island Light has a very deep, interesting, and colorful past. According to one story, the island was named by four men whose ship, the *Increase*, wrecked nearby in April 1682. They appreciated the "boon" of making it safely to the shore of the island that they named it "Boon Island." Another version of the island's name origin states it came from mariners leaving a wooden barrel of supplies (a boon) on the island for shipwrecked sailors who made it to the island so they could survive on the barren rock until they were rescued. Years before the wreck of the *Increase*, Captain John Winthrop details passing "Boon Island" in his sea journal, and there are other references to "Boon Island" as early as 1630.

Boon Island Lighthouse was known as one of the most remote, lonely, and dangerous lighthouse stations in New England. Due to its remoteness, harsh conditions on the island, and frequent storms, most keepers only stayed a few years. The one exception was William C. Williams who stayed at the lighthouse for 27 years and later died at the age of 90.

The original marker for Boon Island was a 50-foot wooden tower built in 1799. The tower only lasted five years before being destroyed in a storm. In 1805, a 40-foot stone daybeacon was built to replace the wooden tower which lasted until 1811, when it was deemed a manned lighthouse was necessary. That year, a new 32-foot lighthouse was built on the island, and a manned station was officially established. The height of the original lighthouse was increased in 1832, although the exact new height is unknown.

In 1855, a new granite tower was built to replace the original lighthouse which was badly deteriorated. The new lighthouse measured 25 feet in diameter at the base, 12 feet in diameter at the top, and 133 feet high, making it to this day the tallest lighthouse in New England (although not the highest light above sea level). At that same time, a new duplex keeper's house was built. The keeper's house was rebuilt in 1899, adding a second story. In 1904, a third keeper's dwelling was constructed to house the second assistant keeper and his family, who, until then, lived with either the head keeper's family or the first assistant keeper's family.

Boon Island Light postcard, 1915-1930, NA.

Boon Island Lighthouse remained manned until the blizzard of 1978, the final chapter of the lighthouse's history as a manned light. During the blizzard, two Coast Guardsmen were manning the light. The violent storm tossed boulders all over the island, flooded the keeper's house with five feet of water, and washed several stones that made up the tower itself out to sea. It damaged the helicopter pad, generator building, house, and fuel tanks, and completely destroyed the boat launch and boathouse.

The only place of refuge for the keepers was in the lighthouse tower, where they remained until they could be rescued by helicopter. Two years later, in 1980, the light was automated, and the damaged home was burned in 1981. In 1993, the second-order Fresnel lens was removed and put on display in the Kittery Historical and Naval Museum and was replaced with a more modern optic.

STORIES

Boon Island Light- Changing Hands

Boon Island: Independent Nation
The 1710 wreck became the foundation for a novel later written by Kenneth Roberts called *Boon Island*. In 2000, the Coast Guard licensed the lighthouse to the American Lighthouse Foundation (ALF), and in 2003 president Timothy Harris, in a spoof attempt to raise money for the ALF, launched a campaign called "The Republic of Boon Island," an idea taken from Roberts book, declaring Boon Island an independent nation and himself as "The Regent Lord Master." The ALF then sold citizenship papers as well as political appointments to raise money for the organization, gaining local and national attention. Unfortunately, Harris left the ALF in 2007, and the organization ended the creative and humorous fundraising campaign.

In 2012, Boon Island Light was offered to the ALF free of charge by the federal government, declaring the lighthouse as "excess property" under the National Historic Lighthouse Preservation Act. Yet, the ALF refused the offer, stating it would be too expensive for the organization to maintain.

Private Ownership
In 2014 the lighthouse was auctioned to the highest bidder and sold to a private individual, Art Girard of Portland, for $78,000. In December 2014, only months after purchasing the lighthouse, he sold it to Boon Island LLC, owned by Bobby Sager, for $119,673. Sager, a lighthouse enthusiast and philanthropist, also purchased Minot's Ledge Lighthouse in 2014, and Michigan's Grays Reef Lighthouse in 2016.

Increase

In 1682, a trading vessel, *Increase*, wrecked on the island and had four survivors. They were marooned on the island for a month, surviving by eating fish they caught and bird eggs. They created a fire in hopes that someone on the shore, just 6 miles away, would see the smoke, and eventually, Native Americans atop Mount Agamenticus did, leading to their rescue.

Cannibalism and the *Nottingham Galley*

In late December 1710, the British merchant ship *Nottingham Galley* was coming from England, headed to Portsmouth, New Hampshire, loaded with three tons of Donegal butter and three hundred wheels of Donegal cheese. The ship sailed into a violent winter storm and wrecked on Boon Island. The crew escaped the sinking ship and made it onto Boon Island but lost most of their cargo in the wreckage. They were marooned on the exposed, barren island and left with little food or supplies to build a shelter or fire.

Two crewmen built a makeshift raft out of wood they salvaged that drifted onto the island but died while trying to reach the mainland, which was within sight 6 miles away. The remaining crew had barely any supplies to build a shelter or fire. They eventually ran out of food on the barren island and ate seaweed and any mussels they could find among the rocks. Two more crew members, including the ship's carpenter, perished from starvation. The remaining crew members had to resort to cannibalism to survive.

Those who survived the 24 days of cold, windy, and often violently stormy weather were finally rescued in early January. It is said that mainlanders found one of the bodies of the men who died trying to reach the shore by raft and went to search for any remaining crewmembers.

This incident played a major role in building a beacon and, eventually, a lighthouse on Boon Island. In the 1990s deepwater archaeologists recovered several cannons, cannonballs, lead shot, fishing weights, and other items believed to be from *Nottingham Galley*. These items currently reside with the Maine Historic Preservation Commission.

Tragedy Rebuilding the Stone Daybeacon

On August 25, 1805, the men who had been rebuilding the daybeacon (the second structure) on Boon Island completed their work but were unable to reach the U.S. Revenue Cutter waiting for them just off the island with their small boat due to the heavy surf. The men were forced to wait on the island two more days until the 27th when the surf had decreased to attempt to reach the Cutter again. Ellis Damon, the contractor for the job, along with his son and the other eight workers boarded the small boat to attempt to reach the Cutter. A heavy sea came along and capsized the boat, tossing all aboard against the breakers and into the sea. Damon, his son, and one other worker drowned, and the others aboard were able to reach the rocks and survived. The Cutter returned to Cape Neddick to get two more boats and rescued the survivors from Boon Island the following day.

Vanishing Vessel

In 1817, keeper Eliphalet Grover reported he was awoken at 2am by his dog barking and went outside where he heard cries for help. He found a small two-masted vessel on the southern part of the island pushing off shore but was quickly pushed back onto shore, fighting the wind and waves. Keeper Grover went to get his two sons for help at which time the vessel appeared to be free. Around half an hour later, he heard a distress call again and he and his sons launched their boat and began to row in the direction of the cries for help using a lantern to light their way. By the time they reached the area where the calls were coming from the vessel had disappeared. The last thing he heard was "come out quick with your boat," and he assumed the boat had sank, although no wreckage was discovered at daylight.

BOON ISLAND LIGHT

Empire Knight

The ledges near Boon Island have claimed other victims since the *Nottingham Galley* and *Increase*. February 11 1944, the 428-foot British freighter *Empire Knight* hit the nearby underwater Boon Island Ledge during a storm. The ship broke in half, killing all 24 sailors aboard. They were unable to reach Boon Island, which was three miles away due to the rough, stormy winter seas.

The freighter had been carrying wartime supplies, including almost 20,000 pounds of mercury. Divers were able to recover some of the mercury, although it is estimated that 16,000 pounds remain in the ship. Diving and salvage attempts near the wreck are prohibited.

Gold Hunter & Hazel E. Ritcey

Winters have always been harsh on Boone Island. During the winter of December 1892, keeper William C. Williams had to rescue the crew from the British Schooner *Gold Hunter*, which had wrecked on the island. The men had to row hard for six hours to reach the island, and the barking of the dog on board woke keeper Williams and his assistants. With temperatures of four degrees below zero, Williams and his assistants rescued the six crewmembers, stating afterward they were, "almost equally incapacitated by exposure." The men were frozen to the thwarts of the yawl boat but all recovered. In 1919, schooner *Hazel E. Ritcey* struck a rock near the island and sank. Keeper Harry Smith, along with his two assistants, rescued the seven men aboard.

Keepers and their wives gather at the base of the lighthouse. n.d., NA.

BOON ISLAND LIGHT

William C. Williams (far right), his wife Mary Abbie Williams (seated, dog at her feet), their son assistant keeper Charles Williams (second from right), with family and/or friends. Early 1900s, William O. Thomson.

Keeper William C. Williams

Longest Lightkeeper on Boone Island

William C. Williams became second assistant keeper on August 5, 1885, making $450 per year. He was promoted twice and, in 1888, became head keeper at $760 per year. He stayed on for 27 years, until 1911, making him the longest keeper at Boone Island, and he never received another raise. He wrote,

"There were days when I first went on station that I could not get away from the idea that I was locked up in a cell... When rough weather came we didn't know as it would make much difference as to whether we went into the tower or not...When the terrible seas would make up and a storm was in the offing, I was always thinking over just what I would do in order to save my life should the whole station be swept away...I believe it is these things which gradually wear on the mind and finally upset the brain."

Happy Thanksgiving

The evening before Thanksgiving Day, 1890, Keeper Williams was inside the tower fretting about what he and his family would have for a meal the following day, as provisions were low at the station. Suddenly, he heard a loud crash on the deck outside and went to investigate. A flock of black ducks had miscalculated their course and had crashed into the tower, leaving eight dead ducks on the lantern deck and four more on the rocks below. Ask, and you will receive; fresh duck for Thanksgiving sounded fantastic to the hungry family!

More Shipwrecks

The first shipwreck Williams remembers during his stay on Boon Island was the schooner *J.H. & G. Perkins*. The vessel ran aground on the northwest side of the island. Luckily for the crew, the wave that pushed them onto the island pulled them back off as it returned to the sea, and they went on their merry way. Four years later, the schooner *Pathfinder* ran aground in the same place, although it was stuck on the island until the next high tide came in and raised it back up. That same year, the schooner *City of Ellsworth* ran aground on the southeast point of the island. It was carrying lumber from Bangor and headed to Plymouth, Massachusetts. This vessel wasn't so lucky- the entire cargo was lost, but the crewmembers survived.

Williams' Worst Storm

On January 31, 1898, the worst storm keeper Williams had ever seen struck. Winds gusted up to nearly 100 miles per hour, creating monstrous waves that crashed against New England's tallest tower, coating the walls with a thick layer of ice. Two four-ton water tanks were destroyed when they were pushed off their granite foundations by the waves and moved 75 feet up the island. Granite boulders weighing upwards of 15 tons were pushed 20 feet or more. Two of the outbuildings on the island were completely swept away, and the fires inside the house went out after the chimneys became completely covered over in ice.

Keeper Williams wrote of the account, "*It was a dangerous piece of work, and the chimneys were cleared only after a hard struggle. But it was a case of clearing out the flues or starve, for the whole house was an iceberg and as for that matter the whole island was the same. It was the hardest night we ever passed, and no one slept on the island during the entire night. The island in the morning was one of the grandest sights I ever witnessed.*"

Other Lightkeeper Stories

Reported Deceased

In 1816 Eliphalet Grover became lightkeeper for a yearly salary of $400. In 1818, he was declared deceased through letters written by three of his enemies. On November 11, Grover sent a letter to the Collector of Customs at Boston Harbor, Henry A.S. Dearborn, a customs officer who was also in charge of managing New England lighthouses and their keepers. The letter stated, *"I have just been informed...that I am dead, but I am ye alive and hope to live to see those people brought to justice for making the report..."* He actually died in 1855.

Message in a Bottle

One story claims that, due to several consecutive weeks of storms and rough seas, the keepers were marooned on the island and running low on food and supplies. They put a message of their despair in a bottle and tossed it out to sea in hopes someone on shore or a passing boat would find it. Eventually, one did. A passing schooner found their message and anchored near the island and waited for low tide, making the distance between the shore and their boat shorter. They then put food in a mackerel barrel, sealed it shut, and set it adrift towards the island. The barrel landed in a small cove and the keepers were able to retrieve it, saving them from starvation.

Life on Boone Island- Tough Times

In a 1932 newspaper article, one lightkeeper from Boone Island shared that you need to know a lot more than how to run a lighthouse to live on Boone Island. He stated that one has to become a *"doctor, painter, steeplejack glazier, boatman, gasoline engineer, electrician, stonecutter, and even a cook when the women folks leave us in the fall."*

Assistant keeper Howard Gray who worked under headkeeper Harold Hutchins explained that they would only get mail and groceries once a month. The service cost them $10 each time, which was a lot during the depression.

Miriam (Dolby) Hammel was the wife of a Coast Guardsman during World War II. They were stationed at Boone Island and she described the freshwater system. Rain was collected from the roof where seagulls would sit all day (lots of poop). The water ran through drainpipes into the cistern in the cellar, which had floating green algae an inch thick on top of it. She noted they boiled every bit of the water they used.

Life on Boone Island- A Different Perspective

Not everyone recalls their time spent on Boone Island to be endless challenges, especially the children and grandchildren who came to the island. Keeper Williams' granddaughter Mary Luther spent many of her summers on the island, and recalls rollerskating on the boardwalk, looking for critters in tide pools, and Sunday picnics.

Assistant keeper Roger Philbrick's daughter Eva was on the island from 1913 to 1917 and remembers playing on the rocks and imagining the seals as her army, and passing whales as her own personal submarine. Keeper Harold Hutchins' daughter Shirley felt like her time there was paradise. She said there was always something to do on the island, and loved being able to fly kites whenever she wanted because there was always a sea breeze.

Legends of Boone Island

There is one legend about the Boon Island lighthouse which claims that sometime during the 19th century the lightkeeper died while on the island. His wife had to take over tending the station and did so until she went mad from the loneliness. She was eventually picked up by a rescue ship, which found her wandering aimlessly around the island.

Shitty Experiences

In the early 1930s, Florence Batty lived on Boon Island with her husband Fred, assistant keeper, and their family. She recalled that instead of indoor toilets, the three families that lived there would cut the tops off of 5-gallon kerosene oil tins and place them in the outhouse as toilets.

During one particular storm, Florence's daughter, Arothusa, went to use the outhouse. Florence heard shrieks from the outhouse and dashed out to see what had happened. Apparently, a rogue wave from the storm had smashed into the outhouse, knocking the windows out and rocking the structure. Arothusa was hovering above the tin can at that moment, which was two-thirds full, and when the wave crashed into the outhouse, it knocked the can over, and its contents spilled all over her, including her hair. Arothusa used the chamber pots inside after that experience.

Florence recalled another incident not long after that same storm. Headkeeper Harold Hutchins set a teapot on the stove and, while waiting for it to heat up, went to use the outhouse. Again, it was storming out, but this time, the waves toppled over the entire outhouse and washed it out back onto the high rocks. She stated, "*I was glad to get off that place. I was scared out in that place...It was an awful life.*"

Aerial view of Boon Island showing the dangerous rocks surrounding the island, 1956, USCGHO.

BOON ISLAND LIGHT

GOAT ISLAND LIGHT

Other Names: Cape Porpoise Light
Location: Cape Porpoise Harbor, Cape Porpoise
Tower Height: 25 feet
Focal Plane Height: 38 feet
Year Built: 1833, 1859
First Lit: August 1833, 1859
Fog Signal: Fog bell, currently automated fog horn, 1 blast every 15 seconds
Past Optics: Lamps and reflectors (1833), fifth-order Fresnel lens (1859)
Present Optic: 300mm VLB-44
Range: 12 nautical miles
Characteristics: Flashing white every 6 seconds
Year Automated: 1990
Year Deactivated: n/a
Status: Active aid to navigation
Keepers: John Lord (1833 – 1841), Thatcher Hutchins (1841 – 1845), Oliver Freeman (1845 – 1849), George Fletcher (1849 – 1853), Samuel Grant (1853 – 1857), George W. Averill (1857 – 1861), Joseph Huff (1861 – 1868), Stephen Ilsley (1868 – 1873), Bradbury Emerson (1873 – 1878), John Emerson (1878 – 1887), Leander White (1887 – 1888), George W. Wakefield (1888 – 1921), Leo Allen (1921 – 1926), James M. Anderson (1926 – 1939), Justin A. Foss (1939 – 1942).

Coast Guard Keepers: Melcher F. Beale (1946-), Joseph Bakken (1946 – 1950), Robert McWilliams (1950 – 1953), Bruce Jordan (1953 –), Lavaughn Bryant (c. 1958-1962), Clifton W. Cousins (1962 – 1964), Edward A. Warren (1964-1965), Wallace R. Potwin (1965-1967), John P. Reidy (1966 – 1967), David M. Sweet (1967), Dennis V. Wilson (1967-1969), Robert L. Haley (1969 – 1970), Charles H. Worrell (1970 – 1973), Richard Heon (1973), Mark D. Brooke (1973 – 1975), Martin Cain (1976 – 1978), Mark Estey (1978 – 1980), Larry L. Toler (1981 – 1983), Bradley Culp (1985 – 1990).

Goat Island Light, c. 1857, NA.

Visit: A distant view of the lighthouse can be seen from Cape Porpoise Memorial Park at the end of Pier Road. The best views are by boat, and there is a dock on the island that is only accessible for two hours before or after high tide. Only the grounds are open, but sometimes during the summer months resident keepers give tours of the tower. New England Eco Adventures out of Kennebunk offers two tours, one that passes by this and other lighthouses, and one that docks on the island with a guided tour.

HISTORY

Goat Island Light was built in 1833. The original lighthouse and 1.5-story keeper's house were built of rubblestone, and the construction was poor. Inspector I.W.P. Lewis visited the lighthouse station in 1842 and noted the mortar used was of poor quality, resulting in cracks in the walls and a leaky roof in both structures. The keeper's house also had rotten cisterns and a bad foundation, making the walls so cracked that the house was uninhabitable in the winter months.

Keeper Thatcher Hutchins (1841-1845) noted the leaks in the lantern room were so bad he had to wipe the glass down three times each night. He had no place to store his boat and had to pay $6 each year to rent the barn on the island for his livestock.

It wasn't until 1859 that the lighthouse and keeper's house were rebuilt. The new tower was built of brick, and the new 1.5-story wooden keeper's house was attached to the lighthouse by a covered walkway. A fifth-order Fresnel lens was installed in the new tower the same year. In 1905, a wooden boat house was built, and in 1907, a brick oil house was added to the station.

The fog bell was replaced by an automated horn in 1959. The Coast Guard began making plans to automate the lighthouse in 1976, but locals heavily petitioned them not to. A local fisherman stated, *"There's a man up there, and we know he watches out for us. A machine can't do that."* Their petitioning worked, and the Coast Guard held off automating the light until 1990. The Goat Island Light became the last lighthouse in Maine to be automated and one of the last in the United States.

The Kennebunkport Conservation Trust has had control over the station since 1992, and has been working since then to restore it back to its 1950s period appearance. In 2011, the fog bell tower and walkway that had been taken in a 1978 storm were both rebuilt.

STORIES

Forty-Six Shipwrecks

Logbook records from keepers on Goat Island between 1865 and 1920 documented 46 shipwrecks in the area, with 28 of them being total losses. The Goat Island region is dangerous due to the many underwater ledges and small islands surrounding the lighthouse. There was a total of 229 people aboard the 46 wrecked vessels, and not a single person perished. Although not all of them were rescued by the lightkeepers, a vast majority were.

The Ghost of Dick Curtis

Caretakers remain on the island despite the light being automated. Richard "Dick" Curtis started caretaking for Goat Island in 1994. He died in a boating accident in May 2002, and his best friend, Scott Dombrowski, took over as caretaker on the island after his death.

Goat Island Light aerial view, c. 1970s, USCGHO.

GOAT ISLAND LIGHT

Dick Makes His Presence Known

Scott invited a friend of his to visit the island one year who brought a woman with him. When she first reached the island, she stated that it was haunted. Scott replied, "I hope so!" in response, missing his best friend. After the tour of the station and lighthouse, the woman told Scott that Dick would "make himself known electronically" when he was around.

Sometime later, Scott had a group of people come to the island for dinner. At one point, the dinnertime conversation died down, and suddenly, the fan above the stove, which was across the room from everyone, turned on. Scott said every time he would land on the island he would walk to the same spot on the beach and, regardless of what the weather was, the fog horn would blast once when he reached the spot. He said this happened for about three years.

Dick Turns Up the Heat

Scott recounted another time when the Flying Santa was coming to visit that Dick made his presence known. Since Scott's kids were older, he would pick up young kids from the mainland and shuttle them to the island to meet Santa. This particular day was very cold and windy, and after shuttling all the kids to the island Scott was really cold and tired. He sat down in Dick's recliner and said: "Dickie if you're here give me some heat." The electric heater in the living room which had not worked in years suddenly turned on. Scott said he warmed up and fell asleep in Dick's recliner; the heater never worked again.

Dick Loves Flags

Scott also said Dick was "flag crazy," and anytime someone from another country would come out to visit, he'd buy the flag of their country and fly it to celebrate their visit. In 2007, President Bush hosted President Putin at Walker's Point. Scott bought a Russian flag and an American flag and put them side by side pointing toward the Bush compound. He said the message was meant to be "we gotta get along," as the two countries did not at the time. After finally getting the flags straight to his satisfaction, Scott asked his friend Dick what he thought about the flags and the fog horn started going off. It didn't stop going off for the next two years. The Coast Guard installed nine new fog detectors in that span of time, and at one point, totally disconnected the power, and it was still going off. It wasn't until the Coast Guard replaced the entire unit that it stopped sounding all the time. ⚓

GOAT ISLAND LIGHT

WOOD ISLAND LIGHT

Location: Wood Island, Saco River, Biddeford Pool
Tower Height: 47 feet
Focal Plane Height: 71 feet
Year Built: 1807, 1839, 1858
First Lit: 1808, 1839, 1858
Fog Signal: Fog bell, currently horn, 2 blasts every 30 seconds
Past Optics: Lanterns & reflectors, fourth-order Fresnel lens (1858)
Present Optic: VLB-44
Range: 18 nautical miles (white), 16 nautical miles (green)
Characteristics: Alternating white and green lights every 10 seconds
Year Automated: 1986
Year Deactivated: n/a
Status: Active aid to navigation
Keepers: Benjamin Cole (1808 – 1809, died in service), Philip Goldthwaite (1809 – 1832, died in service), Tristam Goldthwaite (1832 – 1833), Abraham Norwood (1833 – 1841), John Adams (1841 – 1845), Jotham Perkins (1845 – 1849), Stephen P. Batchelder (1849 – 1853), Nathaniel Varrell (1853 – 1856, died in service), Lyman F. Verrill (1856 – 1857), James R. Bryant (1857 – 1861), Ebenezer Emerson (1861 – 1865), Edwin Tarbox (1865 – 1872), Albert Norwood (1872 – 1886), Thomas H. Orcutt (1886 – 1905), Charles A. Burke (1905 – 1914), Clifford B. Staples (1914 – 1917), Wilbert F. Lurvey (1917 – 1923), Albert Staples (1923 – 1926), George E. Woodward (1926 – 1934), Earle E. Benson (1934 – 1951).

Coast Guard Keepers: Edwin R. Duquette (1952), Forrest S. Cheney (1952), Edward G. Frank (1952 – 1956), Gerald E. Ryan (1957), David A Katon (1957 – 1959), Laurier Burnham (1959 – 1962), Jack B. Netherwood (1962 – 1963), Dave K. Winchester (1963 – 1964), David P. Bichrest (1964 – 1967), John P. Reidy (1966-1967, as temporary/relief keeper), Alfred J. Savageau, Jr. (1967 – 1968), Ronald A. Handfield (1968), James J. Roche (1968 – 1970), Cliff Trebilcock (1970 – 1972), Andrew Pruneau (1972), Jerry Murray (1973 – 1976), Michael McQuade (1976 – 1979), Russ Lowell (1979 – 1982), Paul V. Sodano (1982 – 1983), Phillip Brothwell (1983 – 1985), John W. Blanchard (-1986), Merton Perry (1986), Warren Rowell (1986).

Wood Island Light, c.1859, USCGHO.

Visit: The tower and grounds are open to the public and are accessible through a tour offered by Friends of Wood Island Lighthouse at woodislandlighthouse.org. The station can also be seen from the end of Main Street in Biddeford Pool.

HISTORY

Wood Island is two miles from the mouth of the Saco River, and the town of Biddeford Pool is further upstream. Sawmills and textile mills were built along the river in the 1600s, and there were many imports and exports, mainly lumber and fish, from both the towns of

Biddeford and Saco to the north. In 1806, Congress appropriated $5,000 to build a lighthouse on 35-acre Wood Island. That same year, eight acres were purchased on the island, and Benjamin Beal and Duncan Thaxter, subcontractors for Winslow Lewis, were awarded the building contract for the station.

The first lighthouse was 45 feet high, octagonal, built of wood, and had a shingled exterior. The wooden keeper's dwelling was constructed at the same time. Both were completed by September 1, 1807. The lamp room of the lighthouse used lamps and reflectors and was first

Wood Island Light, n.d., NA.

lit in 1808. It is unclear why the lighthouse wasn't put into use immediately upon completion like most other lighthouses. The lighthouse stood half a mile across the island from the boat landing where supplies were delivered. By 1835, the tower and dwelling were both deteriorating, and the lighthouse rocked so badly that it had to be continually shored up to keep the lantern room level, according to John Chandler, collector of customs and local lighthouse superintendent in Portland.

In 1839, a new 44-foot rubblestone lighthouse and 1.5-story keeper's dwelling were built for $5,000 by J. Berry of East Thomaston. The new lighthouse was circular, measuring 20 feet at the bottom and tapered to 10 feet at the top. The lantern room consisted of two different levels, the bottom being a revolving "eclipser" apparatus attached to a clockwork mechanism that had to be wound up, and ten lamps and reflectors on the top level. The rotation of the light created a flash at set intervals.

Unfortunately, both structures were built very poorly, and the clockwork eclipser often stopped working from dust and dirt binding up the gears and giving the light a fixed appearance, making it easily confused with the light on Goat Island, creating a hazard to mariners. By 1841, the plaster was coming off the walls, and the windows and chimneys leaked. The ever-critical inspector I.W.P. Lewis wrote a report in 1843 documenting the dilapidated state of the lighthouse and dwelling, but it wasn't until after the formation of the Lighthouse Board in 1852 that changes would take place.

In 1854, Congress appropriated another $5,000 to rebuild the lighthouse and keeper's dwelling. While the buildings were under construction, the characteristic of the lighthouse was changed to red so it would no longer be confused with other lighthouses in the region. The new 47-foot tower was built of stone and connected to the new 1.5-story wooden keeper's dwelling by a covered walkway, completed by 1858, along with a fog signal tower. A fourth-order Fresnel lens was installed in the lantern room. It is possible that the "third" lighthouse was actually just a major renovation of the second lighthouse instead of a brand new rebuild,

Wood Island Light, keeper and dog, n.d., NA.

WOOD ISLAND LIGHT

Wood Island Light new tower and dwelling aerial view, 1944, Ralph Eshelman, USLHE.

based on the records at that time stating, "Important repairs have been made..." in regards to Wood Island Light.

In 1868, a boat house and 150-foot boat slip were built. In 1873, a wooden pyramidal fog bell tower was built and was fitted with a steel 1,315-pound fog bell and Stevens' striking apparatus. The machinery would alternate between a single and double blow every 25 seconds. In 1890, the badly corroded steel bell was replaced with a 1,200-pound bell. The old bell was stuck in the ground upside down and was used as a flower planter for several years. In 1892, a barn was added to the station, and a 60-foot plank walk was built. In 1903, an oil house was built.

In 1950, the station was electrified and powered by generators, and eventually, an underwater cable was run from the mainland to the island. Sometime during the 1960s, the fog bell fell into the sea after the framing was destroyed in a storm. It was recovered later and was placed in a museum. In 1966, the keeper's dwelling was expanded through the addition of a second story. In 1972, the Fresnel lens and lantern room on top of the lighthouse were removed and replaced with a rotating aerobeacon. The public complained about the "headless" lighthouse enough that in 1986, when the lighthouse was automated, a new aluminum lantern room was placed back on top of the lighthouse, which was installed by helicopter.

The fog bell was brought to the mainland in 1976 and left on the lawn of the harbormaster. For reasons unknown, not long after, the Coast Guard decided to give the bell to a museum in Delaware. Local residents wouldn't allow their bell to be taken away to Delaware, so they chained it to a tree. Senator Edmund Muskie had to get involved to settle the dispute, and the Coast Guard agreed to let the townspeople keep their bell. It was moved to the grounds of the Union Church before being transferred to Vines Landing, where it stands today.

In 2003, a local chapter of the American Lighthouse Foundation was formed, called Friends of Wood Island Lighthouse. The group works to restore the lighthouse and all structures at the station.

STORIES
Changing of the Keeper Disputes

In 1841, John Adams took over the keeper position for Abraham Norwood. During his time at the lighthouse, Norwood built a stone wall and barn and installed a fence on the property. He also took it upon himself to make part of the dwelling a "cow house" and pigsty. When Adams took over, Norwood demanded compensation for the improvement investments he had made in the property, including $200 for the barn and 50 center a rod for both the stone wall and fence. Adams kept a cow at the station, and Norwood returned to the island after his service ended and harvested the hay that grew on the property. He then charged Adams $14 per ton for the hay. It wasn't uncommon in the early years of lighthouse stations for keepers to build structures on the property and demand that following keepers pay them compensation for the improvements. Some keepers would pay the former keepers, and others, like John Adams, refused.

Ebenezer Emerson

Ebenezer (Eben) Emerson was keeper on Wood Island from 1861 to 1865. On March 16, 1865, around 1 a.m., he woke up to go trim the wicks in the lantern room. It was very windy and foggy that night, although somehow, over the heavy surf's crashes, he heard cries for help out in the water. Emerson attempted to launch the station's boat, but the rough seas were too strong for him to do so alone. He quickly ran to the nearby home of a fisherman, who helped him get the boat in the water and row towards the sounds.

Upon reaching Washburn Ledge, the men saw the brig *Edyth Ann* of Nova Scotia run aground. The crew were hanging on to the vessel's rigging for dear life as the huge winter waves battered the ship, already having carried away one of the ship's lifeboats. Emerson boarded the brig and instructed the crew to get in the remaining lifeboat which hung from the davits over the side of the ship. While aboard, he found two guinea pigs below deck that he put in his pockets, then returned to his own rowboat. Once all the men were in the lifeboat, he waited for a large wave to rise close to the bottom and yelled at the men to set it free. It landed perfectly on the crest of the wave, and the lifeboat rode the wave away from the brig and ledge, saving all of the men aboard just before the vessel broke apart and was smashed to kindling against the ledge. The Canadian government was so thankful for keeper Emerson's heroic rescue that they awarded him a plaque and a pair of brass binoculars.

Smallpox Scare

On December, 25, 1872, the schooner *Cora Van Gilder* ran onto the rocks near Wood Island Light. The master, his wife and child, a mate, and a seaman aboard landed the small boat from the schooner on Wood Island around 6 a.m. that morning. It was 15 below zero, and keeper Albert Norwood was asked to take in the wife, who was freezing to death. The captain brought his wife and child into the lighthouse and sat them down in a chair by the fire.

Keeper Norwood removed the woman's shawl only to discover she had smallpox. Not wanting to spread the disease to his family, he immediately instructed the captain to help him load her into a sled, and they brought the woman to a summer home that wasn't in use half a mile away. Norwood left them with provisions to keep them comfortable and sent for a physician to come to the island. In a letter written on December 27, 1872, from inspector William Mayo to the Lighthouse Board defending keeper Norwood for letting a woman infected with smallpox into the lighthouse, he states that the lightkeeper was told she was "a woman freezing to death" and, considering she was out *"in a biting, bitter cold no man could refuse such an appeal."* He goes on to say *"These big hearted coast watchers identify themselves with such suffering."* The woman eventually recovered, keeper Norwood and his family did not contract the disease, and he was not reprimanded for taking the woman in.

Thomas H. Orcutt & Sailor

Thomas H. Orcutt, a veteran captain from Brooklin, was keeper from 1886 to 1905 at Wood Island. Orcutt brought a 2-month-old puppy he named Sailor to the island during his time as keeper. It was a custom for steamships passing by the lighthouse to salute the light with the sound of their bell or whistle and the keeper to answer back by ringing the bell. One day in 1894, a passing tug boat whistled three times, but keeper Orcutt did not hear the call. Sailor heard the salute and ran to get Orcutt's attention, but he did not hear his dog howling. The dog tried a few more times to get Orcutt's attention with no luck, so Sailor "took matters into

Thomas H. Orcutt with Sailor ringing the bell at Wood Island Light station, n.d., Orcutt Family Photo, Friends of Wood Island Lighthouse.

his own mouth," so to speak! The dog ran to where the bell hung, grabbed the rope attached to the bell's clapper, and rang the bell vigorously in answer to the vessel. The self-taught bell ringer continued to ring the bell from that day on. Sailor was quite well-known, locally and far away, and his story appeared in several newspapers throughout the country including as far away as Georgia, Iowa, and Wisconsin.

Sailor was said to have human-like intelligence, although described as merely a black mutt. He was also a good delivery dog, carrying letters and other small items in his mouth. In 1900, Orcutt said, *"Sailor and I are old comrades. Wood Island would indeed be a lonely place if I hadn't the dog to keep me company. He is a bright, intelligent companion and is perfectly content to live the life of a lighthouse keeper away from all dog friends."* Thomas Orcutt died in 1906 at the age of 72, and Sailor died in his arms just a few months earlier.

Murder-Suicide: Tragedy on Wood Island

Howard Hobbs was a fisherman in his early twenties when he lived on Wood Island. He lived in a chicken coop that had been converted into a makeshift dwelling with another fisherman, William Moses, who was also in his early twenties. On June 1, 1896, the two young men took a boat to Old Orchard Beach and reportedly were drunk upon their return to the island that afternoon. Upon returning to the island that afternoon, the men were greeted by Frederick Milliken, who told Hobbs he wanted to speak to him, sources say, about overdue rent. Milliken was a 36-year-old man of large stature and a fisherman, game warden, and special policeman. He lived with his wife and three children on Wood Island.

Hobbs and Moses went back to their shack, where Hobbs grabbed his rifle and told Moses he was bringing it because he might find some birds to shoot, and the two men headed back to talk to Milliken at his property. Milliken, apparently sensing something may go wrong, greeted them at the garden gate out front. Upon seeing the rifle, he asked Hobbs if it was loaded, who replied that it was not. Milliken, not trusting Hobbs' response, decided to check the rifle chamber himself to verify his answer. When he started walking forward, Hobbs pulled the trigger, shooting Milliken in the chest.

Isabel, his wife, who was also concerned about the state of the two young men, had been watching the entire encounter from the doorway and rushed out to help her husband get inside and onto a bed. Hobbs left, and Moses and Milliken's stepson quickly rowed to shore to get a doctor. Meanwhile, Hobbs went to the lighthouse station near his shack and found Thomas Orcutt in the keeper's dwelling. He told keeper Orcutt what had happened, and Orcutt told him to turn himself in to the authorities. Milliken died within 45 minutes of the gunshot from loss of blood. Hobbs, unable to face what he had done, returned to his shack, where he shot himself in the head.

Wood Island Light aerial view, 1956, USCGHO.

Cursed Island

Many believe that Wood Island is cursed and/or haunted, and not just because of the murder-suicide. Another fisherman who lived an isolated life on the island left for Saco, got a hotel room that was above the first floor, and jumped from a window to his death. Robert Thayer Sterling wrote in his 1935 book *Lighthouses of the Maine Coast and the Men Who Keep Them,* *"Thirty or more years ago, Wood Island was having lots of shipwrecks, and for a time, one would have thought they were specializing in them."* He writes that one winter, three schooners heading to Boston with cordwood from St. John were caught in a winter gale and crashed into Wood Island, with some of the crew perishing.

Coast Guard Years

The Bensons
Earle Benson, a World War I veteran, became head keeper at Wood Island Light in 1934 and was the last civilian keeper. He joined the Coast Guard when it became in charge of lighthouses in 1939 and continued to be the head keeper at the station until 1951. Earle and his wife Alice were previously stationed at Portland Head Light, where there was a nearly constant flood of tourists, and they enjoyed the more peaceful island lighthouse station with fewer visitors. In 1950, the Coast Guard brought electricity to the station, and the couple were happy to upgrade from using a battery-powered radio to a television. They watched the 1950 World Series and enjoyed episodes of *The Lone Ranger*.

A Close Call
Laurier Burham was a keeper from 1959 to 1962. In late November 1960, his two-year-old daughter Tammy fell ill and needed to be transported to the mainland. The seas were rough and a 30-foot lifeboat was dispatched from a nearby Coast Guard station to pick up the girl. By the time the boat reached the island and dropped anchor, it was dark. Two 19-year-old crewmen navigated the rough, dark waters to the lighthouse boat, landing in a small skiff to pick up Tammy. After picking up the small child, they headed back towards the larger boat when a wave caught the skiff broadside and capsized it, dumping all three of them into the rough, churning sea. One of the crewmen was able to swim back to the larger boat, while the other, Edward Syvinski, clung on to little Tammy for dear life despite being hauled underwater repeatedly. He was eventually able to swim them both to a small nearby island.

Although it was too dark to see what had happened, keeper Burnham sensed trouble and launched his even smaller peapod to search the dark, treacherous waters for his daughter. He eventually found Syvinski and his daughter on the island, loaded the two into his peapod, and made it to the 30-foot Coast Guard boat. The girl was then safely transported to shore and fully recovered at the hospital.

It wasn't until 1993, when Tammy was 35, that the Coast Guard recognized the heroic acts of the men involved and issued Commendation Medals to Syvinski, Burnham, and local lobsterman Preston Alley for their bravery in the rescue effort of Tammy. Alley was a lobsterman out of Biddeford who met the 30-foot Coast Guard boat in the harbor at Biddeford Pool and braved the rough seas to bring her to the dock where her grandparents were waiting to take her to the hospital. Alley was deceased when the medals were awarded, but his widow received the medal on his behalf.

Christmas Cheer
Between 1963 and 1964, David Winchester and his family were stationed at Wood Island Light. Determined to give his family a merry Christmas on the lonely island, Winchester bought a tree on the mainland and transported it to the island with the station's boat. He then dragged it up the hill to the boardwalk, loaded it into a cart attached to a small tractor, and drove it over the 1/2-mile boardwalk to the keeper's house.

Peanut Butter Jar Medicine Delivery
Cliff Treblicock was a keeper from 1970 to 1972. He recalled one year when his son fell ill and was in need of penicillin, but it was stormy, and the seas were too rough for him to take the station's boat to the mainland and back to get the medicine. A local lobsterman was willing to brave the treacherous seas and

"THIS BEATS COMMUTING. When you wake up in the morning you're already at work," says David Winchester, 27, who is spending first Christmas as keeper of lighthouse at Wood Island, Me. His wife Pat and children, Robyn, 9 months, and Richard, 4, watch as he unloads Christmas tree. (AP)

The Boston Globe, *December 24, 1963.*

Left: Jessica playing on the Wood Island Light boardwalk. Right: Susan, Jerry, and Jessica Murray with Kelly. **Hartford Courant,** *July 4, 1977.*

retrieve the medicine for Treblicock, although, upon his return, he could not safely get close to the island. Instead, he put the medicine in an empty peanut butter jar, fastened it to a life preserver, and set it afloat towards the island. When the package was within reach, Treblicock used a gaff to hook it and hauled it to shore.

Family Life Alone on an Island

Jerry Murray, his wife Susan "Sam," and their daughter Jessica were stationed at Wood Island Light and the only inhabitants from 1973 to 1976. Murray had dreamed of becoming a lighthouse keeper and was excited when he received a 4-year assignment to Wood Island. Jerry said in a 1976 news article, "*In the dead of winter when an 80 knot wind is whipping the sea up near the tower and the island is a solid sheet of ice you realize you are really on your own...*" Jerry, 26, and his wife Sam, 25, were the only two people present to celebrate Jessica's 4th birthday on the island, who entertained herself playing by on the boardwalk and with her imaginary sister.

The family also had a Collie mix named Kelly, who was brought to the island as a puppy by former Coast Guard keeper Cliff Treblicock between 1970 and 1972. Kelly's job was to keep the mice and rats on the island in check. Jerry stated, "*Kelly goes with the light, I don't think she has been off island more than once or twice for a quick trip to the vet. The dog has been a good companion for our 'Messy Jessy.'*" Kelly stayed at the lighthouse and lived with the following Coast Guard family who came to take care of the light, the McQuades. Jerry's wife Sam loved their time at Wood Island Light, saying, "*To experience the pleasure of living on your own island, surrounded on three sides with a view of open sea and the most glorious sunrises you can imagine is great.*" ⚓

CAPE ELIZABETH LIGHTS
(EAST TOWER & WEST TOWER)

Other Names: Two Lights, Twin Lights
Location: Cape Elizabeth
Tower Height: 67 feet (both towers)
Focal Plane Height: 129 feet (East tower), 130 feet (West tower)
Year Built: 1811 a single 50-foot tall rubblestone unlit daybeacon, 1828 two 65-foot rubblestone towers, 1874 present towers
First Lit: 1828, 1874
Fog Signal: Fog bell (1834), steam fog whistle (1869), now only the east tower has an automated horn with two blasts every 60 seconds
Past Optics: Lamps and reflectors (1828), second-order Fresnel lens (1855, the East tower's lens is on display at Maine Maritime Museum in Bath)
Present Optic: FA-251 (1994)
Range: 15 nautical miles (original), 17 nautical miles today
Characteristics: Four white flashes every 15 seconds
Year Automated: East tower- 1963
Year Deactivated: West tower- 1924
Status: East tower- active aid to navigation & private residence, West tower- deactivated, private residence
Keepers (East & West):
Head: Elisha Jordan (1828 – 1834), Charles Staples (1834 – 1835, died in service), Ebenezer Dyer (1835 – 1841), George Fickett (1841 – 1844), Hiram Staples (1844 – 1849), William Jordan (1849 – 1853), Ivory Jordan (1853), Nathan Davis (1853 – 1859), Milton Libby (1859 – 1861), James Mariner (1861 – 1869), Enoch Dyer (1869 – 1872), Hezekiah Long (1872 – 1873), Marcus A. Hanna (1873 – 1888), Leander White (1888 – 1909), William F. Stanley (1909), Frank L. Cotton (1909 – 1926), Joseph H. Upton (1926 – 1934, died in service), Edward D. Elliot (1934 – 1946).

First Assistant: William L. Willard (1854 – 1855), Charles Peables (1855), William D. Murray (1855 – 1856), J.M. Higgins (1856 – 1857), Samuel Black (1857), T.T. Richards (1857 – 1859), H. McKenney (1859), Caleb L. Gould (1859 – 1861), Michael Staples (1861 – 1869), James Lowe (1869 – 1872), James E. Dyer (1872 – 1873), James Lowe (1873), Enoch Murray (1873), Albus R. Angell (1874 – 1875), Harry S. Libby (1875 – 1881), Albus R. Angell (1881 – 1887), James W. Sterling (1887 – 1888), Fernando Wallace (1888 – 1889), William H.H. Wyman (1889 – 1890), Ira D. Trundy (1890), Charles M. Griffin (1890 – 1893), Ira D. Trundy (1893 – 1894), Frank L. Cotton (1894 – 1902), Henry M. Cuskley (1902 – 1903), Frederick A. Stone (1903 – 1905), Byerly S. Stanley (1905 – 1906), William P. Richardson (1907 – 1919), James M. Anderson (1919 – 1926), Robert T. Sterling (1926 – 1928), Andrew H. Kennedy (1928 – 1929), Alton S. Cheney (c. 1930 – 1935), John H. Olsen (1935 – 1944).

Second Assistant: B.F. Libby (1859 – 1860), James Boucher (1860 – 1861), Eugene E. Whitney (1861 – 1863), William D. Staples (1863 – 1864), Enoch Dyer (1864), John Brown (1864 – 1867), **Martha W. Mariner (1867 – 1868)**, **Susan H. Mariner (1868 – 1869)**, Allen Gatchell (1869 – 1871), T.A. Staples (1871 – 1872), James E. Dyer (1872), **Abbie H. Long (1872 – 1873)**, James Dyer (1873), Enoch Murray (1873), William H. Hanna (1873-1874), James T. Hanna (1874 – 1877), John W. Williams (1877 – 1878), Joseph W. Girty (1878 – 1880), Charles E. Chase (1880), Albus R. Angell (1880 – 1881), Hiram Staples (1881 – 1886), William C. Williams (1886), Fernando Wallace (1886 – 1888), Thomas H. Ingersoll (1888 – 1889), Ira D. Trundy (1889 – 1890),

Charles M. Griffin (1890 – 1891), George E. Staples (1891 – 1892), Wolcott H. Marr (1892), Frank L. Cotton (1892 – 1894), Harry Phillips (1894 – 1897), George P. Wood (1897), William A. Stetson (1897 – 1898), Henry M. Cuskley (1898 – 1902), John W. Cameron (1902), Fred H. Hodgkins (1902 – 1903), Edward T. Merritt (1903 – 1905), Byerly S. Stanley (1905), William P. Richardson (1905 – 1906), Allen C. Holt (1907 – 1912), Alonzo Morong (1912 – c. 1915), James M. Anderson (1917 – 1919), Robert T. Sterling (1919 – 1926), William F. Dawes (1929 – 1945).

Third Assistant: N. Hibbard (1859 – 1861), Francis A. Staples (1861 – 1864), Charles W. Staples (1864 – 1869), Enoch Murray (1869 – 1872), Enoch Murray (1873), James E. Dyer (1873), William H. Hanna (1873), Nathaniel J. Hanna (1873-1874), **Louie (Louisianna) A. Hanna- wife of head keeper Marcus Hanna (1874 – 1888)**, Frank H. Peabbles (1888), John O. Philbrick (1888 – 1889), Joseph C. Knight (1889), Frank C. Strout (1889), Charles M. Griffin (1889 – 1890), George E. Staples (1890 – 1891), Wolcott H. Marr (1891 – 1892), Frank L. Cotton (1892), Albert H. Willard (1892 – 1894), Harry Phillips (1894), George P. Wood (1894 – 1897), William A. Stetson (1897), Henry M. Cuskley (1897 – 1898), Charles M. Griffin (1898 – 1901), John W. Cameron (1901 – 1902), Fred H. Hodgkins (1902), Joseph M. Austin (1902), Arnold B. White (1902), George W. Joyce (1902 – 1903), Byerly S. Stanley (1903 – 1905), William P. Richardson (1905), Allen C. Holt (1905 – 1906), Arnold B. White (1907 – 1909), Alonzo Morong (1909 – 1912), Joseph H. Upton (1912 – c. 1913), Will A. Clark, Jr. (1915 –), Augustus A. Wilson (1917), Lennie (Leonard) Foster (c. 1919 – c. 1924).

Coast Guard Keepers: Clifton S. Morong (1946 –), William H. Woodward (1946 – 1947), Arthur R. Marston (c. 1946 – 1947), Robert Power (1947), John L. Mason (officer in charge, 1952-1957 and 1959-1962), Clifton Morong (1946-1955), Joseph Bakken (c. 1953), William Luttgeharm (c. 1954), James R. Wilson (c. 1966).

Visit: Since both properties are privately owned, the only way to see the two lights is by boat, air, or from the road. The best public spot to view the twin towers is The Lobster Shack Restaurant, at the end of Two Lights Road in Cape Elizabeth, next to the fog signal building.

CAPE ELIZABETH LIGHTS (EAST TOWER & WEST TOWER)

HISTORY

In 1811, the first navigational aid was built in Cape Elizabeth. It was a 50-foot rubblestone daybeacon, which was painted black on the top and white on the bottom. As marine traffic continued to increase, it was decided that two lighthouses should be built in place of the daybeacon. The two towers and keeper's house were constructed of rubblestone in late 1828, but it was so cold that the mortar froze, and every time it rained, the water would run in between the rocks, keeping the structures constantly wet on the inside.

Elisha Jordan was the first lightkeeper, and his wife, although her name is not listed, was the first assistant keeper. Jordan and his wife were keepers of the light until 1834, when politics cost him his job. He was replaced by Charles Staples, who had sold the land to the government to build the towers. His salary was increased by $50 that year when the first fog bell was added. The following year, Staples died of cancer.

In 1843, George Fickett was lightkeeper when engineer I.W.P. Lewis came to inspect the lights. The towers and dwellings were badly deteriorated. The mortar was even worse; the roofs and walls leaked, and the wood was rotting. There was no cistern for fresh water, the west tower's light mechanism was defective, and the fog bell could only be heard over the crashing waves when there was an offshore wind. The lightkeeper didn't have a boat to get from one tower to the other and instead had to walk the 895-foot distance between them, making it especially difficult when snow filled the valley between the two lights.

At that time, Stephen Pleasanton was the Treasury official in charge of light stations. He was known for being a penny-pincher, and during his time in charge of light stations, several lightkeepers, including Fickett, recanted their statements regarding the disrepair of their homes and stations, most likely from threats or bribery from Pleasanton. Fickett went so far as to claim that the woodwork was in good shape, there were no leaks, and he'd always had a large boat. This happened often enough that the Lighthouse Board grew suspicious and conducted its own inspections. They discovered that many light stations were in terrible states of disrepair, which prompted them to take over responsibility for all lights.

In 1852, keeper William Jordan wrote to the board stating that he had to hire extra help to keep up with the duties at the light stations, as it was too much for one man. At that time, he was paid $500 per year and requested an additional $100 per year to cover the wages of his hired help. In 1854, the board appointed an assistant to the station, and in 1859, second and third assistant positions were added to keep up with operating and maintaining the two lighthouses.

In 1854, a new fog bell was installed, and the old bell was brought to Portland Head. In 1855, the eastern tower received several improvements, including lining the interior with bricks, a cast-iron staircase, and a new lantern. That same year, the west light was extinguished, and the east light was given an occulting third-order lens. This only lasted eight months, and in 1865, the west tower was given a large red vertical stripe and the east tower four red horizontal bands.

Both towers at Cape Elizabeth, late 1800s, NA.
CAPE ELIZABETH LIGHTS (EAST TOWER & WEST TOWER)

In 1869, a steam fog whistle was installed, and in 1875, a second-class siren was added. In 1883, the west light was extinguished again, but it was relit shortly after due to many complaints. In 1886, a 32-foot square fog signal building was built across from the lifesaving station. In 1888, it was recorded that its signals sounded for 1,117 hours in total, using 71,500 pounds of coal. In 1901, the siren was replaced by a second whistle. In 1929, the fog signal was changed to an air diaphone, which proved terribly loud for nearby residents, and a silencer on the exhaust pipe was installed.

In 1874, two new matching 67-foot cast-iron brick-lined lighthouse towers were built, sitting 923 feet apart. The towers had elegant Italiante details and were painted brown. The second-order Fresnel lens stayed in the west tower, and the east tower received a new first-order Fresnel lens.

A new wooden 1.5-story keeper's house was built in 1878, and the original stone keeper's home was repaired. The head keeper's family lived in the new home, while the second assistant keeper lived in the repaired stone keeper's house, and the first assistant keeper lived in a wooden home near the west tower. In 1890, the stone house was replaced with a wooden one. By 1888, four families were living at the stations, and by 1901, the house near the west tower was expanded so it could house the families of the first and third assistant keepers.

In 1924, the east light was changed to a flashing white incandescent light. That same year, the government made the decision to change all twin light stations to single light stations, and that was when the west tower went dark permanently. The west tower's second-order Fresnel lens was modified and placed in the east tower, producing 17 seconds of light followed by six flashes every 30 seconds. In 1927 and 1929, American painter Edward Hopper painted Cape Elizabeth's Two Lights, and his oil painting, *The Lighthouse at Two Lights*, was put on a U.S. postage stamp in 1970.

1970 stamp painted by Edward Hopper.

The west tower was used as an observation post during World War II, and a cylindrical turret was installed at the top of the tower. In 1959, the tower was auctioned to the highest bidder, actor Gary Merrill, the ex-husband of Bette Davis, for $28,000. He sold it in 1983. The keeper's house near the east tower was eventually sold in 1999, and the new owners remodeled and expanded the structure, making it look vastly different from the paintings done by Hopper and upsetting many locals and historians who appreciated its original charm.

In 1963, the east light was automated, and its 1,800-pound second-order Fresnel lens now resides in the Maine Maritime Museum in Bath. In 1997, the Coast Guard received the new Keeper-class buoy tender *Marcus Hanna*, named after a keeper at Cape Elizabeth Light Station from 1873 to 1888 in honor of the heroism he had displayed during his time in service. The Keeper-class of Coast Guard cutters consists of 14 different ships, all named after heroic lighthouse keepers. Its home port is in South Portland. The east light continues to be maintained by the Coast Guard, and the tower is licensed to the American Lighthouse Foundation.

Aerial view of both towers, 1953, USCG.
CAPE ELIZABETH LIGHTS (EAST TOWER & WEST TOWER)

STORIES

Marcus Aurelius Hanna

The Cape Elizabeth Lighthouses are the first "twin" lighthouses built on the coast of Maine. Between 1780 and 1990, at least 98 vessels wrecked on the shores of Cape Elizabeth. Known to be a treacherous spot even by the most experienced of captains, the twin Cape Elizabeth Lighthouses hold some of the most commendable rescue stories among Maine's lightkeepers.

A Daring Rescue

Marcus Aurelius Hanna was appointed lightkeeper by President Ulysses S. Grant from 1873 to 1888. In the winter of January 28, 1885, Hanna had a terrible cold. He finished his fog signal shift in *"one of the coldest and most violent storms of snow, wind and vapor... that I have ever witnessed."* He was so worn down from his illness and the weather that he had to crawl through the snow in negative ten-degree temperatures back to the keeper's house.

Marcus Hanna, n.d., USCG.

Not long after he fell asleep, his wife "Louie," the station's third assistant keeper, noticed a wrecked schooner out in the harbor and woke her husband for assistance. The *Australia* had hit a ledge, and the storm dragged the captain and cargo out to sea. Two crewmen clung to the rigging, getting drenched by the waves. They were nearly frozen from the cold, harsh winter storm wind.

The seas were so rough that Hanna was unable to launch a boat to come rescue the crewmen. The wreck was close enough to shore that Hanna figured he could throw the men a line and drag them through the icy waters to safety. The only problem was that he would have to climb over large, ice-covered rocks to get close enough to the men. He knew if he fell, he would land in the ice-cold pounding surf and be dragged out to sea as well, but he felt an obligation to try and save the crewmen, no matter how dangerous it was. Hanna stated, *"I felt a terrible responsibility thrust upon me, and I resolved to attempt the rescue at any hazard."*

He tied a wrench to a rope for weight and made attempt after attempt to get the rope to the stranded men, with no luck. He knew he had to get closer to the men, and the only way to do that was to wade into the ice-cold water. Everyone knows the ocean is cold, but the ocean in the winter is an entirely different type of cold. I found myself in a similar situation one frigid March, although no one's life was at risk, just a boat. What follows is my personal experience to give you some perspective on how Hanna must have felt.

Author Angela's Story

It was the winter of 2014-2015, the year the Eggemoggin Reach froze completely over near the Deer Isle Bridge. I was on a small lobster boat that was being test-driven for the first time that year. The ice had broken up finally and we launched at the boat ramp beside the bridge. Not long after passing under the bridge, the boat ran out of fuel. Always make sure your boat is full of fuel, especially if it's March and there are no other boats around. We drifted aimlessly until we ended up in a cove. The cove was filled with thick sheets of ice stacked up on one another. We finally came safely to rest and were able to get off the boat once the tide dropped low enough.

The small cove was on the Sedgwick side, not far from the bridge. We knew the boat wasn't going anywhere until the tide came back up, so we walked through the woods to the main road and crossed the bridge on foot (not advisable, as there is no sidewalk on the bridge, but we didn't have a choice). We grabbed the truck, a few cans of fuel, drove back, parked in a nearby driveway of a family we knew, and headed back down to the shore.

The captain jumped back up on the boat from the rocks, and I stayed on shore. The plan was to throw me the anchor so I could toss it in between some rocks at the point of the cove, and then the captain was going to use the pot hauler that hauls up lobster traps to drag the boat out to the point where the water was deeper. After several futile attempts to reach the rocks, just like Hanna, I, too, knew what I had to do. I waded into the freezing cold water to get the extra distance I needed to throw the anchor.

The second the water hit my legs, all I could feel were pins and needles on my skin. I kept going until I was up to my waist, threw the anchor, and missed again, but I was much closer this time. I knew I couldn't last long in the water and tried again, making sure this toss counted. My second toss was a success. The anchor lodged firmly between the rocks at the point, and the captain began hauling the boat out into deeper water. I immediately got out of the water and struggled back to the truck, barely able to walk from the nearly hypothermic feeling I had from the waist down. Once in the truck, I hauled off my soaked pants, boots, and socks and drove home with the heat cranked and half naked. Good thing I didn't get pulled over...that was definitely an adventure I'd rather never repeat!

Back to Marcus Hanna's Story
I can imagine how Hanna felt, already battling an illness and wading into the frigid waters to save these two men. After a few attempts, Irving Pierce caught the line, tied it to himself, and Hanna hauled him to shore through the pounding surf and over ledges. The ship was starting to break up, and Hanna knew there wasn't much time left. He tossed the line to the second crewman, Bill Kellar, who was able to grab it. Hanna was near collapse at this point when assistant keeper Staples and two neighbors showed up and helped haul Kellar to safety.

Both crewmembers recovered, and Hanna was awarded the Gold Life Saving medal that year for his heroism, and in 1895 he was awarded the Congressional Medal of Honor for his bravery during the Civil War. Hanna is the only person in history to ever receive both of these awards. Not to mention to also have a Coast Guard ship named after him!

Joseph Upton
In January 1934, 65-year-old keeper Joseph H. Upton set off around 9:30 pm for the station's east tower to light the auxiliary light because the main light had malfunctioned. Two hours later, his wife awoke and noticed he hadn't returned. She phoned the tower but was unable to reach him and went to look for him. She found him unconscious with a fractured skull at the base of the east tower, apparently from a bad fall. He was sent to the Portland hospital but passed away the following day. People have claimed they've seen the ghost of Upton, an older man in a lightkeeper's uniform, at the station.

Cape Elizabeth, late 1800s, NA.
CAPE ELIZABETH LIGHTS (EAST TOWER & WEST TOWER)

PORTLAND HEAD LIGHT

Location: Cape Elizabeth
Tower Height: 80 feet
Focal Plane Height: 101 feet
Year Built: 1791
First Lit: 1791
Fog Signal: 1,500 lb bell (1855), 2,000 lb bell (1870), fog trumpet (1887), now horn, 1 blast every 15 seconds
Past Optics: Lamps and reflectors, fourth-order Fresnel lens (1855), second-order Fresnel lens (1864), fourth-order Fresnel lens (1883), second-order Fresnel lens (1885), aerobeacons (1958)
Present Optic: DCB 224 airport aerobeacon (1991)
Range: 24 nautical miles
Characteristics: Flashing white every 4 seconds continuously
Year Automated: 1989
Year Deactivated: Remained a manned station but went dark from June 1942 to June 1945 during World War II
Status: Active aid to navigation, museum
Keepers:
Head: Joseph K. Greenleaf (1791 – October 5, 1795, died in service), Reuben Freeman (1795-1796), Dave Duncan (1796), Barzillai Delano (1796 – 1820, died in service), Joshua Freeman (1820 – 1840), Richard Lee (1840 – 1849), John F. Watts (1849 – 1853), John W. Coolidge (1853 – 1854), James S. Williams (1854), James Delano (1854 – 1861), Elder M. Jordan (1861 – 1869), Joshua F. Strout (1869 – 1904), Joseph W. Strout (1904 – 1928), John W. Cameron (1928 – 1929), Frank O. Hilt (1929 – 1944), Robert T. Sterling (1944 – 1946).

Assistant: G.E. Jordan (1864-1865), William D. Staples (1865 – 1866), William A. Adams (1866), Charles S. Jordan (1866 – 1868), William D. Staples (1868 – 1869), **Mary E. Strout** (1869 – 1877), Joseph W. Strout (1877 – 1904), John W. Cameron (1904 – 1928), Millard Urquhart (1928), Robert T. Sterling (1928 – 1944).

Coast Guard Keepers: William T. Burns (1944 – 1954), Archie McLaughlin (- 1946), William L. Lockhart (1946-1950), William T. Burns (1946-1956), William F. Yost (c. 1950), Earle E. Benson (1951 – 1954), Howard Beebe (– 1952), Archie McLaughlin (c. 1954 – 1957), Edward G. Frank (1956 –), Henry E. Leonard (1957 – 1960), Carl Salonick (c. 1959-1961), Weston E. Gamage, Jr. (1961 – 1962), Chester E. Candage (1961-1962), David J. Beaster (1962-1963), Walter A. Dodge (1963), Robert L. Moody (1963),

Portland Head Light showing the shorter tower, original dwelling, and fog bell tower, c. 1859, NA.

PORTLAND HEAD LIGHT

Portland Head Light as seen from Delano Park showing new dwelling, 1891 or after, USLHS.

James R. Wilson (1963-1964), Armand E. Haude (1963 – 1965), William C. Guilford (1964-1965), Clifton M. Wood (1965-1966), Manford H. Durkee (1965 – 1967), Raymond L. Schmitt (1966), Thomas M. Reed (1966 – 1967), John H. Johnson (1967 – 1968), Franklin D. Allen (1968 – 1974), Kenneth A. Perry (c. 1973-), Roy B. Cavanaugh (1974 – 1977), Tony DiNardi (1975-), Jerry Poliskey (c. 1977-), Victor L. Bissonnette (1977 – 1978), Gregory Clark (c. 1978-), Raymond W. Barbar (1978 – 1982), Marion P. Danna (1980 – 1983), Michael W. Cook (1982 – 1986), Nathan Wasserstrom (1986 – 1989), Davis Simpson, Jr. (1986 – 1989).

Visit: This lighthouse can be visited on the mainland. It is located at Fort Williams Park off Shore Road in Cape Elizabeth. The park is open year-round, and the museum is open Memorial Day through Indigenous Peoples Day Monday-Friday 10-2 and Saturday & Sunday 10-4.

SPECIAL NOTE: This lighthouse usually participates in Maine Open Lighthouse Day, where, for one day only every year, the tower is open to the public. Due to how popular Portland Head Lighthouse is that day, <u>only 300 tickets are typically available</u> on a first-come, first-serve basis, and you must be 48" tall. **These tickets are given out <u>when the park opens at daybreak</u>, and they are gone before the lighthouse opens!**

Portland Head Light showing the Daboll trumpet (left) and three diaphragm horns with the largest in the center, n.d. NA.

HISTORY

By the 1790s, Portland had become the sixth busiest port in America. Maine was still part of Massachusetts in 1784 when 74 merchants petitioned the government for a lighthouse to be built at Portland Head to aid mariners entering Portland Harbor. Following the deaths of two people in a shipwreck in 1787 off Bangs (Cushing) Island near Portland Head, the colonial government finally agreed to build the lighthouse.

The Massachusetts colonial government was poor and could only appropriate $750 to build the rubblestone lighthouse and keeper's dwelling, which was underway by August 1789. Jonathan Bryant and John Nichols, both from Portland, were the masons heading the project, which originally called for a 58-foot-tall tower. After a survey was conducted partway through construction, it was realized that the light would not be visible from the south. The plan was changed, requiring the tower to be 72 feet tall. Unhappy with the increased work but no increase in pay, Bryant quit, leaving Nichols to complete both the lighthouse and dwelling on his own.

In the spring of 1789, the federal government was formed, and construction all but stopped. The First Congress passed the Lighthouses Act that same year, giving the federal government control over all lighthouses, which had previously been state-controlled, and appropriated an additional $1,500 to complete the tower. Portland Head Lighthouse became the first tower completed and to go into commission under the newly formed Federal Government under the Lighthouses Act in late 1790.

Portland Head Light was first lit on January 10, 1791, by Revolutionary War veteran Captain Joseph Greenleaf, appointed by President George Washington. The original light consisted of 16 whale oil lamps and reflectors.

There was some debate regarding Greenleaf's pay when he started the position. Some sources state he was not paid for the lightkeeper position and instead was given the right to live in the dwelling and fish and farm the surrounding waters and land. Greenleaf petitioned the President in a letter dated November 24, 1791, stating his "compensation is fixed below the rate at which he can afford to perform the service." This suggests that he did receive pay, with the United States Lighthouse Society stating his beginning salary was $100.

Portland Head Light showing original dwelling and brick fog house with Daboll trumpet, between 1885 and 1891, USCGHO.

Another source states that in June 1792, Greenleaf wrote that he was ready to quit the position as he couldn't afford to stay, and the job was far more difficult than he had expected. He wrote that the prior winter ice formed so thick on the lantern glass that the light couldn't be seen, and he had to melt it on a regular basis. In 1793, the government agreed to pay Greenleaf $160 per year for the position, which he kept until his death. On October 3, 1795, Captain Greenleaf rowed his boat to town to conduct some business. While rowing back to the light station, he fell down in the boat, as observed by those standing on the wharf he had just left. They rowed out to assist him, but he had already passed away by the time they reached him.

Keeper Barzillai Delano, a local blacksmith, became keeper in 1796 at a salary of $225 per year. In 1809, he sent a letter stating that crossing from the dwelling to the tower was difficult as it was very steep and rocky, and during the winter, it becomes even more dangerous as the sea washes over the path and freezes. He requested

Portland Head Light real photo postcard with S.S. Regina passing by, 1900 or after, USCGHO.

PORTLAND HEAD LIGHT

Portland Head Light aerial view, n.d., USLHS.

a passageway be built connecting the two structures, although this wouldn't happen for years. In 1810, an oil shed was added so he no longer needed to store the lamp oil on the floor of the lighthouse, and the woodwork in both the lighthouse and keeper's dwelling, which had rotted over the years, was replaced.

In 1812, an inspection noted the lower 50 feet of the tower were constructed well, but the remaining upper section was built poorly after mason Bryant quit, and Nichols was left to complete the construction alone. Contractor and retired sea captain Winslow Lewis suggested removing the upper 25 feet of stonework and the small five-foot diameter lantern deck and replacing it with a new, larger-diameter lantern deck, lowering the overall height of the tower. In 1813, the poorly built upper section was removed by Winslow and replaced with a new pine deck sheathed in copper, and a new iron lantern deck, 10-foot in diameter, was placed on top of the new timber deck. A new Argand lamp and parabolic reflector system designed by Lewis replaced the old lighting system. In 1816, a new keeper's dwelling was constructed, and outbuildings were attached to the kitchen ell to connect the dwelling to the tower, making passage between the two structures much easier and safer in the winter.

In 1842, civil engineer I.W.P. Lewis, well-known for his overly critical and pessimistic assessments of light stations, visited Portland Head and reported the tower was constructed of poor quality mortar, had rotten woodwork, and the roof leaked. He also noted the keeper's dwelling had cracked walls and was leaking. He recommended removing some of the lamps in the lantern room as he believed there were too many. Upon reading Lewis's report, Richard Lee, keeper at the time, wrote his own response to the assessment. He stated both structures were in good shape and were comfortable. He wrote: "*The tower has been built over 50 years, and is now strong and tight, and will probably remain a good tower for hundreds of years.*"

In 1850, the lantern room and deck were replaced, and a new system of 13 lamps and reflectors were installed. An inspection in 1851 revealed that the reflectors were already scratched, the quality of the oil was bad, the dwelling leaked, rats were undermining the tower, and the keeper, John Watts, had to hire a man for two days to teach him how to run the light since there were no written instructions.

In 1855, the lamps and reflectors were replaced with a fourth-order Fresnel lens, a fog bell tower was built, and a 1,500-pound bell from Cape Elizabeth was installed. That same year, the lighthouse was lined with brick, a cast-iron spiral staircase replaced the wooden one, and a workshop was added. The new Fresnel lens featured a single lamp compared to the old light apparatus using multiple lamps, and oil consumption dropped from 220 gallons in six months to only 48 gallons in six months.

In February 1864, the 295-foot passenger steamer *Bohemian* from Liverpool, England, wrecked on Alden's Rock, four miles from Portland Head, because the captain was unable to see the light from the lighthouse. Forty immigrants aboard the ship perished, and it was decided the lighthouse should be raised back up an additional 20 feet using brick. Following the completion of the addition, a second-order Fresnel lens was installed in the lantern room, making the light visible for 21 miles. In 1864, an assistant keeper was employed to help run the new light and keep up with other duties at the station.

On September 8, 1869, a hurricane knocked the fog bell tower into a ravine and nearly killed the lighthouse keeper. The fog tower was rebuilt in 1870, and a 1,800-pound bell and Steven's striking mechanism were installed. By 1871, Halfway Rock Light was completed, which lies offshore in Casco Bay, and the Lighthouse Board decided Portland Head Light was less important and reclassified it as a harbor light. In 1872, the bell was replaced with a Daboll trumpet from Monhegan Island Lighthouse.

In 1883, the exterior brick building attached to the tower was removed, the tower was shortened by 20 feet, and the second-order lens was replaced with a weaker fourth-order Fresnel lens. The lard oil, which required heating in the colder months, was replaced with kerosene that same year. There were many complaints about the changes made to the lighthouse, and less than two years later, the tower was restored to the original height, and the second-order Fresnel lens was returned, which was relit January 15, 1885.

In 1887, a engine from Boston Light was repaired and brought in to run the fog signal. In 1891, the stone dwelling was removed and a new Victorian-style two-family keeper's house was built, designed by architects Royal Luther and Edward P. Arams. That same year, a new brick oil house was built to store kerosene for the lamp.

From April to July 1898, the lamp went dark out of fear of helping enemy ships during the Spanish-American War. Nearby Fort Williams, built in 1872, was expanded during this time, and padding was added to the exterior of the lighthouse lens to avoid damage from the fort's gunfire. The lighthouse grounds were also off-limits to visitors during this period. Sometime during or after the war the station received much damage from practice fire coming from Fort Williams, including damage to windows, the roof, siding, and chimneys.

In 1900, the lighthouse was renovated, including replacing many of the tower's original stones and extensive repointing. That same year, two oil engines with air compressors were brought in for the fog signal. Around this time, the station was also connected to the town water system.

In 1929, the lighthouse received electricity, and the light's characteristic was changed for the first time, from fixed to two seconds on, two seconds off. In 1938, an air diaphragm was installed in place of the old fog signal, which had three horns. The large horn was pointed toward Halfway Rock Light, and the two smaller ones pointed toward Portland Harbor and the Portland Lightship. The station remained in operation but went dark from June 1942 to June 1945 during World War II and was off-limits to unauthorized personnel.

Aerobeacons replaced the Fresnel lens in 1958. On August 7, 1989, Portland Head Light was automated,

Portland Head Light when the lighthouse was painted as a brown daymark, n.d., USLHS.

PORTLAND HEAD LIGHT

Portland Head Light, n.d., USLHS.

and the keepers were removed. A celebration was held that day as it also marked the 200th anniversary of the establishment of the Lighthouse Service. The lighthouse property was deeded to the town of Cape Elizabeth in October 1993. In 2005, renovations were completed, including repointing and painting the tower, painting the keeper's dwelling, and some windows in the lighthouse were replaced.

STORIES
Interesting Keepers and Experiences

Captain Joshua Freeman, keeper from 1820 to 1840, took great pride in his position. He would sit and watch the ships pass through with a coil of rope at his side, ready in an instant if a shipwreck occurred. It was also said that he was very hospitable to visitors and was known for supplementing his keeper's income of $350 a year by selling rum and other spirits to visitors and local fishermen for three cents a glass. He saved the top-shelf liquor for the local minister.

Frank O. Hilt became head keeper in 1929 and constructed a giant checkerboard near the base of the lighthouse for entertainment. The Flying Santa Edward Rowe Snow and his wife Anna would come out to visit Hilt on occasion. Snow once wrote that he enjoyed photographing his wife and Hilt playing a match on the giant board.

Captain Joshua F. Strout, n.d., Cape Elizabeth Historical Preservation Society.

Privacy was often hard to come by when working at a lighthouse. In the 1950s, Coast Guard keeper Earle Benson reported that a woman let herself into the keeper's dwelling, sat down at the kitchen table, and demanded service. She insisted he and his wife were government employees and, therefore, she was entitled to service. In the 1960s, Coast Guard keeper Wes Gamage's wife got quite a surprise one day when tourists carrying cameras burst into the bathroom upstairs in the dwelling while she was taking a bath. They made sure they locked the doors and windows after that event!

The Strout Family of Lightkeepers
The Beginning of a Long Family Tradition

In the 1820s, Jane Strout, age 16, worked for keeper Captain Joshua Freeman as a housekeeper for the dwelling at Portland Head Light. Although Captain Freeman was married and the keeper's wives typically did the housekeeping, it was possible his wife Eliza was too sick to keep up with the housekeeping work and needed help (Eliza passed away in 1830). It appears that Jane was good friends with Joshua and his wife Eliza because when her first child, a son, was born, she named him Joshua Freeman Strout, after keeper Freeman.

Captain Joshua Freeman Strout started his life on the sea at the age of 11, became a cook on a tugboat by age 18, and began captaining ships in 1854, and captained many vessels throughout his career. He became owner and captain of the brig *Scotland* and traveled as far as Cuba and South America on the ship. While aboard the bark *Andreas*, Strout suffered a severe fall from the masthead and was forced to give up his career on the water. After his fall, Strout took up a position at Portland Head Light in 1869 for $620 per year. His wife, Mary, was appointed assistant keeper that same year and was paid $480 per year. The couple raised 11 children at the station, and during their 35 years at Portland Head Light, three of their sons, John, Charles, and Stephen, were all lost at sea.

Mary resigned in 1877, and the couple's son, Joseph, took over the assistant keeper position. It became a job that nearly killed him when a hurricane hit the region on September 8, 1869. The winds were so forceful that they knocked the fog bell tower over, destroying the structure and almost landing on Joseph.

Joseph W. Strout, son of Joshua, at Portland Head Light. Notice the Daboll trumpet in the background on the brick fog signal station, n.d., Jeremy D'Entremont, Kraig Anderson Inventory of Lighthouse Personnel.

In an interview in 1898, keeper Joshua Strout said he went 17 years straight without taking any time off and hadn't gone past Portland in a two-year stretch. When he retired in 1904, he was the oldest keeper at the time, at 78 years old. He died two years later at the age of 80. Following his retirement, his son, assistant keeper Joseph, became head keeper. Joseph remained in the position until 1928; for a total of 59 years, the Strout family lived and worked at Portland Head.

Wreck of the *Annie C. Maguire*

On Christmas Eve in 1886, the British bark *Annie C. Maguire* crashed into the rocks at Portland Head Light in heavy winter seas brought on by a strong gale in heavy snowfall. At that time, Joshua and his son Joseph were keepers of the light, and Joseph said the storm was so terrible that "even Santa Clause was afraid to be out." The two had been forewarned to keep a lookout for the ship ahead of time as it was wanted because its owner owed debts, and the ship was suspected to be seeking shelter from the storm in Portland Harbor. No one expected the ship to crash in the backyard of the lighthouse!

Upon discovering the ship, Joshua told his son, Joseph, "*There's a ship in the backyard.*" The Strouts jumped into action and rigged a breeches buoy, which looks like a hanging basket with leg holes, from the base of the lighthouse to the cross-tree of the ship. They were able to get everyone in it and pull them from the ship, along with the captain's sea chest, across the ravine and over to shore safely. The survivors were all very cold, and their frozen clothing had to be cut or torn from their bodies. The Strouts grabbed blankets and dry clothing to help warm everyone up, and all were grateful to the Strouts for rescuing and taking care of them that Christmas Eve. Captain Daniel O'Neil, his wife and 12-year-old son Thomas, two mates, and nine crewmen were on board. Anything they could save was removed from the ship, and the *Annie C. Maguire* broke apart in a storm about a week later.

PORTLAND HEAD LIGHT

Wreck of the **Annie C. Maguire** *showing the ravine passengers needed to cross from the ship, c. December 25, 1886, Portland Head Light Museum.*

Captain O'Neil was soon served with a sheriff's attachment for the debt owed, and his sea chest was promptly seized. When the sheriff opened the sea chest, only papers were located inside, and no money. Apparently, Captain O'Neil's wife had the sense to take the money out of the chest before it was shuttled off the ship and place it in her hat box, which she carried with her as she was rescued from the ship.

January 14, 1912, on his 21st birthday, John Strout, son of Joseph Strout, chipped away a flat surface on the rock near where the ship wrecked and painted a memorial inscription of the wreck on the ledge which read "In Memory Of The Annie C. Maguire Wrecked On This Rock, Dec. 24, 1886." The tradition of repainting the inscription still remains today.

Other Strout Family Stories

The Strouts had a macaw named Mickey, who lived at the lighthouse with them. Joshua brought him back from one of his trips to South America when he was captain of the brig *Scotland*. John taught Mickey to say, *"Light the light. Light the light. Fog's rolling in."* Mickey lived to be over 80 and spent his retired years living with Joseph Strout's brother.

Portland Head Light during the automation ceremony with **Nantucket** *lightship offshore, August 7, 1989, Jeremy D'Entremont.*

PORTLAND HEAD LIGHT

Joseph Strout served at Portland Head Light for 51 years and nine days and was known by many as "Cap'n Joe." He happily greeted thousands of visitors each summer, giving them tours of the grounds and lighthouse. His kindness earned the appreciation of many visitors, who would send many gifts and remembrances each Christmas, including fruit from California, candy, and other delicacies and gifts for him and his family.

On July 4, 1952, a ceremony was held at Portland Head Light, and a memorial plaque was placed on the lighthouse, honoring all of the head keepers who had worked there since 1791. The plaque had been a dream of John Strout's, which he was able to see come true. On October 12, 1954, head Coast Guard keeper W.T. Burns invited the Strout family to the lighthouse for a visit. John, his son John, his wife June, and their daughter Donna Lee Strout all climbed the stairs of Portland Head Light, making five generations of Strouts who climbed the winding stairs to the top of the lighthouse.

Tragedy at the Light

On the evening of July 19, 1807, Captain Adams was bringing the schooner *Charles* into Portland when, in a thick fog, the ship ran aground on a ledge near Portland Head Light. The waves breached the ship, and sixteen of the twenty-two passengers, including women and children, were lost. Captain Adams made it to shore with three other men but heard his wife screaming and went back into the sea to rescue her and never returned. One passenger, Eleazer Jenks of Portland, attempted to save his life by lashing himself to the shrouds, although he still drowned and was found still lashed to them.

In the 1870s, a party hired two carriage drivers to take them to Portland Head to watch the waves crash during a storm. The two drivers went too far out on the rocks, were hit by a rogue wave, and swept away. Their bodies were found several days later.

Robert T. Sterling sitting below Portland Head Light, n.d., American Lighthouse Foundation.

Robert Thayer Sterling

Robert Thayer Sterling from Peaks Island was the last civilian keeper before the Coast Guard assumed responsibility for the light station in 1946. He had previously worked as a reporter for several Portland papers covering the news on the waterfront. Through reporting these happenings, Sterling decided he would like to become a lighthouse keeper.

Sterling began his career as a lightkeeper on September 3, 1913, at Ram Island Ledge Light. From there, he transferred to Great Duck Island Light, Seguin Island Light, Cape Elizabeth Light, and finally, Portland Head Light. During his time at Cape Elizabeth Light, Sterling began writing feature articles for local newspapers in his spare time. After being transferred to Portland Head Light, he started writing stories of Maine's lighthouses and completed the book *Lighthouses of the Maine Coast* in 1935. The book contains stories he and other lightkeepers experienced, as well as ship captains, buoy tenders, and others connected to the lighthouse service.

Henry Wadsworth Longfellow

Born in 1807, famous poet and Portland native Henry Wadsworth Longfellow visited Portland Head Light frequently when he was younger. Most believe his poem "The Lighthouse," written in 1849, was inspired greatly by his time spent at Portland Head Light. Longfellow frequently visited the lighthouse during the time Joshua Strout was head keeper, and the two would sit and talk over cold drinks. He usually visited once or twice a week and had a favorite rock on the south side of the tower he would sit on. That rock is now marked by a plaque explaining why the rock is significant and also has several lines from his poem "The Lighthouse."

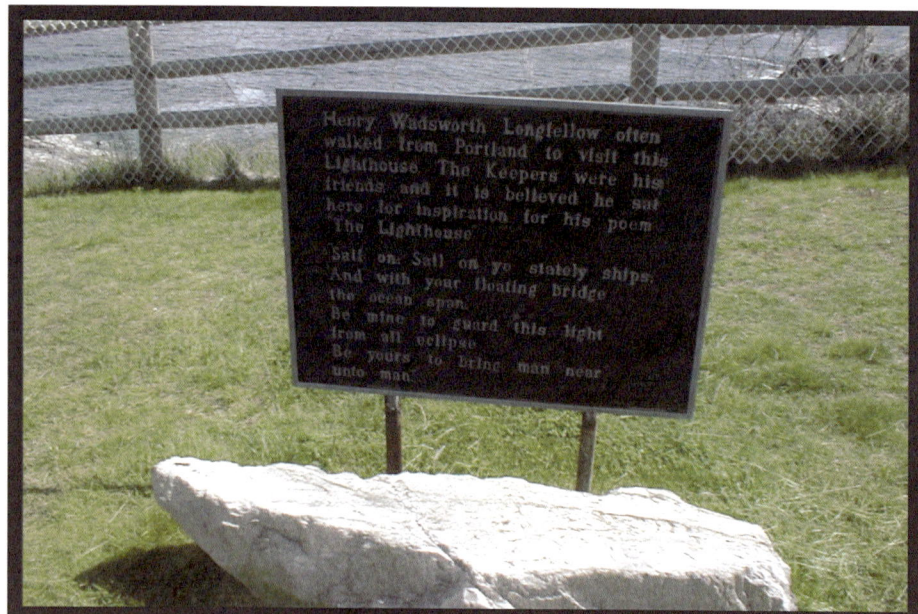

Portland Head Light, "Longfellow's Rock," 2002, Jeremy D'Entremont Collection.

Stormy Weather

In February 1972, a severe winter storm hit the station. It tore the fog bell from the housing, peeled 80 feet of a steel fence out of concrete, and broke a window in the house 25 feet up, flooding the dwelling with seawater a foot deep, along with mud and even starfish!

In March of 1977, a fierce Nor'easter hit the area, knocking out power to the station. The generators were burned out as well, leaving Portland Head Light dark during the storm, the first time since World War II. The storm was so bad that the Coast Guardsmen and their families were evacuated from the station until it passed. ⚓

RAM ISLAND LEDGE LIGHT

Location: Entrance to Portland Harbor, Casco Bay, Cape Elizabeth
Tower Height: 72 feet
Focal Plane Height: 77 feet
Year Built: 1905
First Lit: 1905
Fog Signal: Fog bell (1905), currently horn, 1 blast every 10 seconds
Past Optics: Third-order Fresnel lens
Present Optic: 300mm (VLB-44)
Range: 8 nautical miles
Characteristics: Two white flashes every 6 seconds
Year Automated: 1959
Year Deactivated: n/a
Status: Active aid to navigation, privately owned
Keepers:
Head: William C. Tapley (1905 – 1921), John B. Dewyea (1921 – 1929), Leroy L. Myers (c. 1930 – c. 1939).

First Assistant: Edward T. Merritt (1905 – 1909), Arnold B. White (1909), John C. Morong (1909 – 1913), Edgar W. Lovatt (1913 – c. 1922), Frank William Alley (1926 – 1928), Robert J. Carr (1928 – 1936), Joseph M. Connors (1936 – 1942).

Second Assistant: Wellington M. Latham (1905 – 1908), Wilson G. Joy (1908 – 1909), Joseph A. Rietta (1909 – c. 1912), Edgar W. Lovatt (c. 1913 -), Robert T. Sterling (1913 – 1914), Walter L. Emerson (1914 – 1915), Harry E. Freeman (1915 –), Harry H. McClure (1917), Jaruel B. Pinkham (c. 1919-), Frank William Alley (1920 – 1921), Myron L. Wilson (1923 - 1924), Millard H. Urquhart (1926 – 1927), Robert J. Carr (1927 – 1928), Harry C. Leavitt (1928 –), Lloyd L. McBride (c. 1932- c. 1934), Morris J. Foss (1936 – 1937), Roy N. Cousins (1937 – 1942).

Coast Guard Keepers: William A. Clark (c. 1940 – 1942), Joseph M. Connors (1942), Morris J. Foss (1942 – 1943), Joe Johansen (1949 – 1950), Irving T. Sparrow (1949 – 1951).

Visit: Ram Island Ledge Light can be seen from the Portland Head Lighthouse on land or by boat. Portland Discovery Land & Sea Tours out of Portland offers lighthouse tours around the harbor, where you can see four different lighthouses, including Ram Island Ledge. The grounds and tower are closed.

Ram Island Ledge Light and Fort Levett, view during construction of lighthouse, 1904, Library of Congress.

HISTORY

Ram Island Ledge, located just over a mile from Portland Harbor, is a treacherous rock outcropping about a quarter-mile long that is surrounded by other ledges, many just below the water's surface. It has long been feared by mariners, especially those traveling in the dark, fog, snow, or stormy weather of any kind. As early as 1855, an iron spindle marked the ledge, although it could only be seen during the daytime. In 1873, a wooden tripod standing 50 feet tall was built on the rock, although waves smashing into the ledge and crashing over it washed it away at least three times.

Ram Island Ledge Light construction, c. 1903, courtesy of Dolly Bicknell, USLHS.

Just before midnight on February 24, 1900, the 440-foot transatlantic Allan Line steamer *Californian* left Portland Harbor bound for Liverpool. A strong southeast wind was blowing, making the waves choppy, and blinding snow greatly reduced visibility. Captain John France accidentally drifted off course, and less than an hour after leaving the, the ship struck the ledge head-on, and finally stopped when it became lodged in a hollow in the ledge. The 21 passengers and 96 crewmembers aboard were all rescued, and the cargo, valued at $300,000, was unloaded onto another ship. The steamer was so lodged into the reef that it remained there for six weeks before it could be pulled free. Although the hull suffered damage from the incident, it was not a total loss because the steamer could still float, and was sent to Boston for repairs then returned to service.

The incident brought to light how hazardous Ram Island Ledge was to mariners, especially with the increase in ship traffic to Portland Harbor as the port grew at an incredible rate. The grain trade out of Portland expanded from around one million bushels between 1895 and 1896 to more than 14 million bushels just five years later. The First Lighthouse District took notice and sent an inspector and engineer to assess the ledge.

The report noted that vessels calling at Portland had to pass between Ram Island Ledge and Jordans Reef, which were three-quarters of a mile apart, and Witch Rock, which lies just four fathoms below the water at low tide, being located 1,000 yards in front of the passage, right in the center of the passage. This means all ships coming into Portland Harbor had to navigate between Witch Rock and Jordans Reef or Witch Rock and Ram Island Ledge, and both courses were very dangerous without any navigational aid. The report concluded that a light and fog signal be placed on Ram Island Ledge to assist mariners in safely passing between Witch Rock and Ram Island Ledge.

Ram Island Ledge Light construction, c. 1904, courtesy of Dolly Bicknell, USLHS.

Construction was authorized in June 1902 for the cost of $166,000, but didn't begin until 1903 after the property was

RAM ISLAND LEDGE LIGHT

Ram Island Ledge Light, c. 1905, courtesy of Dolly Bicknell, USLHS.

purchased and the deed secured. Unfortunately, more ships were wrecked on the ledge in the meantime. In September 1902, *Glenrosa*, a British three-masted schooner, became wedged on the rocks after the captain was misled by the sound of the Portland Head Light fog horn. The crew stayed aboard overnight and rowed to shore at daybreak, although the ship couldn't be saved. In December of that same year, the schooner *Cora & Lillian* also crashed into the ledge and was a total loss.

The purchase of the ledge from two Cape Elizabeth families commenced on March 10, 1903 for $500. That same month, the Bodwell Granite Company out of Rockland was contracted to supply granite blocks from their quarry on Vinalhaven island for the construction of the lighthouse. The tower was to be 28 feet in diameter, 70 feet to the base of the lantern deck, and be built of 699 granite blocks set in 35 courses (rows). Its design is a twin to Graves Light in Boston Harbor, which was constructed around the same time.

Work began on May 1, 1903, beginning with cutting down and leveling the site on the ledge where the lighthouse would sit, which was completed by June 30th. The granite blocks, supplied by the Bodwell Granite Company, were cut in a manner that made them fit perfectly together at the quarry shop on Vinalhaven. They were numbered so they could be reassembled in the right order at the ledge, and were transported out to the ledge on two sloops.

Once they reached the ledge, the granite blocks, weighing 4 tons at the base of the lighthouse and three tons near the top, were hoisted using a derrick and hoisting engine mounted to a platform onto the ledge and set in place. The workers were protected from the ocean waves by a 100-foot timber bulkhead that was bolted to the ledge, and temporary living quarters were built on Ram Island, which lies right next to the north side of the ledge, around 600 yards away. Construction of the lower portion of the lighthouse could only take place at low tide since the ledge was completely submerged at high tide.

Each of the granite blocks were secured to the ledge using four large bolts that went into the ledge three feet, and into the blocks eight feet. A 22-foot deep cistern was built in the base of the tower and lined with concrete for freshwater. Work was put on hold on September 30 as the weather began to turn colder and windier, making construction more difficult, and more funds were required to complete the project. By then, the workers had completed 16 courses of the tower, and it was 32 feet high.

The following April work resumed, and the 70-foot granite portion of the tower was completed in July 1904. The granite blocks were lined with enamel bricks on the interior of the tower. A 26,000-pound, 16-foot high iron lantern room manufactured in Atlanta was shipped by rail to Portland to complete the tower that fall. The weather caused additional delays in the completion of the lighthouse until the following spring.

A third-order Fresnel lens was shipped from Paris, France, for the tower, and the kerosene light was first lit on April 10, 1905. It shone two white flashes every six seconds, and the clockwork mechanism that rotated the lens that floated on a bed of mercury had to be wound every hour and a half. The entrance to the tower was located in the galley on the first floor, which started above the cistern that was on the bottom level, and was accessed by a ladder.

RAM ISLAND LEDGE LIGHT

The original plans did not call for a landing pier for the tower, although it was difficult to land men and supplies on the ledge, especially in rough weather. Using surplus funds from the project, an iron landing pier was completed that summer, which stood 18 feet high, 70 feet long, and 20 feet wide. That same year, an oil house and fog bell tower were built on the end of pier. The fog bell went into service on August 28 with striking machinery that hit the bell every 10 seconds.

The station had three keepers who worked on a three-week rotation, with each keeper working two weeks at the lighthouse, followed by one week of shore leave. This way, there were two keepers at the station at all times, woh worked in 12-hour shifts. The station was never fitted with modern conveniences, and lightkeepers had to use a two-hole outhouse located on the pier, which could be unpleasant in rough weather.

In 1958, a power cable ran underwater from Portland Head Light to Ram Island Ledge, and the lighthouse was automated. By then, the Coat Guard was in charge of the light, and the last of their personnel left the lighthouse on January 14, 1959. The light and fog bell were monitored remotely by Coast Guardsmen stationed at Portland Head Light. In 2001, the lighthouse was converted to solar power, and the third-order Fresnel lens was replaced with a 300mm optic.

In 2009, the Coast Guard deemed Ram Island Ledge Light as excess and offered it at no cost to eligible organizations with an interest in maintaining and preserving the lighthouse. They didn't receive any acceptable applications and offered the lighthouse up for auction in June 2010. Ram Island Ledge Light was purchased by Dr. Jeffrey Florman of Windham, Maine on September 14, 2010 for $190,000 and the station remains privately owned today.

STORIES
Lobstering Turf Wars

The first head keeper at Ram Island Ledge was William Tapley. During his time there, the lobster fishermen of Casco Bay sent a petition to the Bureau of Lighthouses requesting that they prohibit lightkeepers from lobstering. Their reasoning was that they felt lightkeepers had an unfair advantage, as they were located in the heart of prime lobster fishing grounds and could tend traps during brief lulls in bad weather, whereas lobstermen leaving the mainland wouldn't be able to reach the fishing grounds and make it back before the seas turned rough again. They also argued that they were only making just enough to get by lobstering and didn't need competition that had an unfair advantage.

Inspector J. McDonald from the Bureau of Lighthouses investigated the claims and discovered that lobstermen made much more than lightkeepers. He sent an inquiry to keeper Tapley in regard to the matter. Keeper Tapley responded: "*I have never owned or hauled a lobster trap, I have not time and do not care to fish. My time is occupied in and around my station, and I prefer to be a light-house keeper rather than a fisherman. The two occupations do not go well together.*" The board's final decision was to allow lightkeepers to fish so long as it did not interfere with their lighthouse duties.

Ram Island Ledge Light aerial view, 1951, USCGHO.

RAM ISLAND LEDGE LIGHT

Dangerous Waters

Just before the lighthouse was completed, on January 12, 1905, a lime coaster, *Leona*, out of Rockland, Maine, that was heading for Rockport, Massachusetts, hit Ram Island Ledge while trying to reach Portland Harbor in a snowstorm. The captain and crew rushed to get off the boat as they knew once the lime came in contact with water, it would ignite. They made it into a lifeboat and rowed for several hours against the storm, and after the captain fired a flare gun, the construction crew on Ram Island saw it and came to their rescue. Once the lime ignited, it burned the *Leona* down to the waterline.

In 1922, two men were in a boat with no compass and became lost in the fog near Ram Island Ledge Light. Keeper Dewyea aided the men in reaching shore. On August 23, 1927, around 10:30 p.m., a man's motorboat wrecked on the ledge in thick fog. The keepers didn't notice the accident, and so, to attract their attention, the mariner lit a mattress that was aboard on fire. Assistant Keeper Frank Alley noticed the blaze and came out to help the man get to the tower where he stayed for the night.

To Own a Lighthouse: Bidding Wars

After the lighthouse was offered up for auction online, several interesting things took place. When the auction entered what is known as the "soft closure" period in early September 2010, at least one bid had to be received every day in order to continue the auction. If no new bids were received between 9 a.m. and 3 p.m. in a single day, the auction would end.

A Brunswick businessman with experience in IT and high-tech image mapping named Bob Muller wanted to keep the lighthouse in Maine hands, so he created a website to solicit others in the state to join him and pay $49 to own a part of the lighthouse as a group. Although he had a great idea, the auction soon surpassed the amount of money he was able to raise from his efforts.

The auction seemed to come down to two men, Arthur Girard, who was a real estate developer from Portland, and Dr. Jeffrey Florman, who was a neurosurgeon from Windham, who collectively raised the price over $100,000. The two men agreed to a coin toss to determine who would continue in the auction, which happened on Friday, September 10, with Florman winning the toss. Girard had placed the last highest bid, and so Florman continued the auction by submitting a bid of $180,000 to top the last bid.

There were still other parties who were interested in the lighthouse who had yet to bid, and they began entering the auction shortly after. On September 13, a bidder with the screen name "arakiran" bid $185,000, and the next morning, a bidder with the screen name "redtide" bid $190,000 just before 9 a.m. Florman, whose screen name was "MAINE" throughout the auction, seemed to have dropped out of the bidding war. Because "redtide" placed their bid minutes before 9 a.m., and no other bids were received by 3 p.m. that day, the auction was completed, and "redtide" won the auction.

As it turned out, "redtide" was a second screen name created by Florman, who now owns Ram Island Ledge Light. Florman, who doesn't even own a boat, is more of a history buff than a lighthouse fanatic and purchased the property merely to preserve the historic landmark. He stated he is: "just a random guy who lives with his family in the woods." Arthur Girard didn't let losing the auction for the Ram Island Ledge Light stop his plan of owning a lighthouse. He went on to win the auction for Boon Island Light in 2014 for $78,000. ⚓

RAM ISLAND LEDGE LIGHT

SPRING POINT LEDGE LIGHT

Location: Spring Point Ledge, Portland Harbor, South Portland
Tower Height: 54 feet
Focal Plane Height: 54 feet
Year Built: 1897
First Lit: 1897
Fog Signal: Fog bell and striking mechanism (1897), currently horn, 1 blast every 10 seconds
Past Optics: Fifth-order Fresnel lens
Present Optic: 300mm
Range: White 12 nautical miles, red 10 nautical miles
Characteristics: Flashing white every 6 seconds with two red sectors
Year Automated: 1960
Year Deactivated: n/a
Status: Active aid to navigation
Keepers:
Head: William A. Lane (1897 – 1901), Harris S. Grant (1901 – 1902), Frank L. Cotton (1902), Charles E.B. Stanley (1902 – 1905), Jerome C. Brawn (1905 – 1906), Otto A. Wilson (1906 – 1931), Augustus "Gus" A. Wilson (1931 – 1934), Leroy S. Elwell (1934 – 1936), Douglas L. Larrabee (1936 – 1942).

Spring Point Ledge Light, 1897, USCGHO.

Assistant: Harry Philips (1897 – 1898), Harris S. Grant (1898 – 1901), Jed M. Johnson (1901), Charles A. Burke (1901 – 1902), Charles E.B. Stanley (1902), Thomas H. Lugersoll (1902), John W. Cameron (1902 – 1904), Jerome C. Brawn (1904 – 1905), Allen Carter Holt (1905), Irving C. Loring (1905 – 1907), Leroy S. Elwell (1907 – 1909), Edward T. Merritt (1909 – 1914), Daniel J. Doyle (1915 – 1917), Augustus "Gus" A. Wilson (1917 – 1931), Douglas L. Larrabee (1931 – 1936), Lester W. Davis (c. 1939 – c. 1941).

Coast Guard Keepers: John Attleson (– 1945), Ralph C. Norwood (1951 – 1954), Joseph Bakken (1954 –).

Visit: The lighthouse can be visited by land on Fort Road in South Portland, near the Southern Maine Community College campus. Portland Harbor Museum and Spring Point Ledge Light are both located on the right. The grounds are open, and the tower is occasionally open, typically on Tuesdays and Thursdays during the summer months.

HISTORY

Spring Point Ledge sits in the main shipping channel heading into Portland Harbor, making it a dangerous obstacle as it sits just under the water's surface at high tide. Many ships hit the ledge, including the lime coaster *Nancy*, on September 7, 1832.

Freighted with a load of lime, which is highly volatile when mixed with water, the vessel struck the ledge, and the hull split in two. The ship began to take on water, which soon started a fire and burned the ship down to the waterline.

After this disaster, mariners petitioned for a marker for the ledge, mainly a lighthouse. However, officials were convinced that the light that was to be built on the Portland breakwater, over a mile away, would be enough for the entire harbor. They agreed to mark the ledge's beginning with a large spar buoy, which was no use at night or in dense fog and did not last throughout the harsh winters. Ships continued to hit the ledge, including the *Mazatlan*, *Seguin*, *Solomon Poole*, *Smith Tuttle*, and many more.

In March 1876, a winter storm produced a heavy gale, making the waters heading into Portland Harbor treacherous. The 393-ton bark *Harriet S. Jackson* was on her way to seek shelter from the storm in the harbor but hit Spring Point Ledge on the way in during the night. The crew remained aboard overnight, and when daylight came, it was low tide, and they were surprised to see that they could lay planks across the scattered rocks and walk to shore. It took two days to remove the grounded vessel from the ledge.

Despite all of the shipwrecks that had already occurred, the Lighthouse Board still wasn't convinced that a lighthouse was needed on Spring Point Ledge. It wasn't until seven different steamship companies collectively petitioned the Lighthouse Board for a light on Spring Point Ledge that they finally listened.

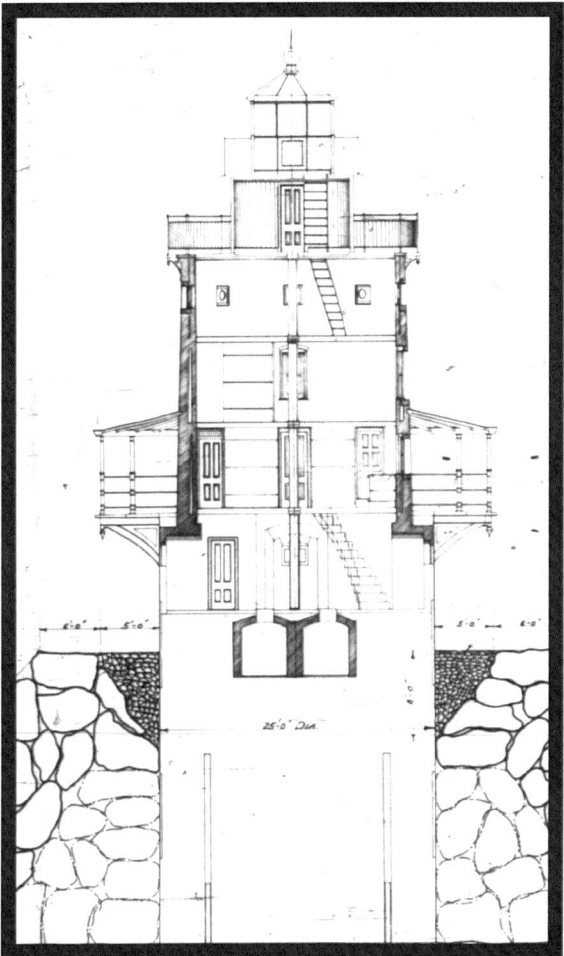

Spring Point Ledge Light cross section, January 16, 1934, USLHS.

The companies argued that together, they carried over 500,000 passengers to Portland every year and that it was only a matter of time before a large-scale tragedy was to occur at Spring Point Ledge due to its dangerous location.

The Board finally responded in 1891, recommending to Congress that a lighthouse be built on the ledge, citing the importance of the harbor for commerce, a refuge from storms, and a growing number of summer visitors to the Portland area every year. Their request initially fell on deaf ears, and the following year, on August 12, 1892, the schooner *Anna Currier* freighted with lumber and bound for Boston crashed into the ledge. The Lighthouse Board petitioned every year for a lighthouse to be built for four consecutive years until, in 1895, $20,000 was finally appropriated to build a lighthouse on Spring Point Ledge. An additional $25,000 was appropriated for the project the following year.

Thomas Dwyer of New York, New York, won the contract to build the sparkplug-style lighthouse, one of only 49 built in the United States, which began in August 1896. A full-time diver was hired to assist in leveling the rock foundation, which sat around 900 feet offshore, and placing the 1.25-inch iron foundation plates, although a terrible storm hit the harbor on September 6, destroying almost all of the progress that had been made. The tower construction was above the waterline by October 25 of that year, and the lantern room was hoisted to the top of the structure in February 1897. The lantern was first lit on May 24, 1897.

The lighthouse was 54 feet tall and had four floors. Unlike most sparkplug lights, which are built entirely of iron caissons, Spring Point Ledge light had a 25-foot diameter iron caisson for the bottom section filled with concrete

Spring Point Ledge Light breakwater construction, 1951, USCGHO.

to the basement floor and a brick upper section. The basement, the top part of the caisson, had two cisterns recessed into spaces in the concrete below, with openings at floor level to collect and store fresh water from the roof. The basement floor space was used as a storeroom for supplies, and an oil room with a 239-gallon kerosene tank was used to fuel the light.

The next level was a first-floor kitchen that housed a hand-pump to the cisterns below for water, followed by a second-floor head keeper's quarters and the third-floor assistant keeper's quarters. Above that was the watch room where the fog bell hung outside, and a lantern room at the very top. Due to the limited space inside the lighthouse, it was a stag station, with the keepers' families living onshore nearby.

Initially, the lighthouse was red, and the lower caisson was painted black, but by November, the lighthouse tower was painted white. The original optic was a fifth-order Fresnel lens that produced a white flash every five seconds, with the white sector marking the channel entrance to Portland Harbor and two red sectors marking where to steer clear of the channel.

Another unique feature of Spring Point Ledge Light was the sector box used to mark the narrow safe passage in the channel, which is typically accomplished with range lights. The sector box was a hollow, rectangular box propped up outside the lantern room to restrict the white sector of the light into a narrow beam of six degrees. Outside of the white sector, it shows all red light. The need for the restrictive sector box became apparent less than three weeks after the light went into operation. The sector box remained in use until the 1980s, when an empty space between two pieces of red glass was used instead.

Early on, a terrible winter produced thick ice sheets that pummeled and damaged the iron caisson. Large granite blocks were stacked around the foundation for additional protection, which proved effective. In May 1898, the lighthouse was closed temporarily after concerns about the potential of an attack on the harbor during the Spanish-American War. The closure didn't last long, as the U.S. mainland did not come under attack.

Due to the lighthouse's close proximity to shore, the keepers would regularly go ashore to see their families and get fresh, home-cooked meals. A storm that lasted from January 27 to 28, 1933, prevented the keepers from going ashore, and they were left with the limited food supply they had at the station for two days.

In 1934, the lighthouse received electricity via a submarine cable from nearby Fort Preble. Another cable ran from Spring Point Ledge Light to the Portland Breakwater Light so it could be remotely operated from Spring Point. A kerosene generator was used for backup should the power from shore fail.

In 1946, the Army Corps of Engineers received approval to construct a 900-foot breakwater from the shore to Spring Point Ledge, although Congress didn't appropriate funds until 1949. The breakwater was constructed of granite blocks weighing between three and five tons each, for a total of 50,000 pounds of granite. The construction cost $200,000, and it was completed in June 1951.

SPRING POINT LEDGE LIGHT

The lighthouse was automated in 1960, and the Fresnel lens was replaced with a 300mm lens. The foghorn was also automated. In 1998, under the Maine Lights Program, the station was transferred to Spring Point Ledge Lighthouse Trust out of Portland Harbor Museum. When the group opened the lighthouse for public tours on May 22, 1999, it became the country's first sparkplug lighthouse open to the public. The inside of the lighthouse was refurnished with period furniture.

STORIES

Augustus "Gus" Wilson

Gus Wilson was keeper at Spring Point Ledge Light between 1917 (as first assistant keeper) and 1934 (as head keeper). He had previously worked at Goose Rocks Light and Two Lights before being reassigned to Spring Point Ledge Light. Gus was a well-known carver of decoys, renowned for their incredible detail and unique head and wing positions. Gus sold his decoys for 75 cents to Walker & Evans sporting goods store in Portland and also gave many away to friends and family. Many of his decoys were carved during his time as head keeper at Spring Point Ledge Light.

Gus carved more than game birds; his collection included African animals and smaller marsh birds that he saw on the Maine coast. Around 1940, his carvings became very popular collectors' items. Some can be found in museum collections, while others ended up in private collections. Many of his carvings sold at auction and fetched anywhere from hundreds to thousands of dollars- one decoy sold in July 2005 from a Cape Cod barn for $195,000. In April 2006, two more of his decoys were discovered in a fish shack in Cape Porpoise and sold for $148,000 and $150,000.

Missing Lens

The original fifth-order Fresnel lens from the Spring Point Ledge Lighthouse vanished after it was automated. In 2016, the Coast Guard, through the U.S. Department of Justice, filed a lawsuit to recover the lens. Chairman of the Spring Point Ledge Lighthouse board of trustees Keith Thompson researched the whereabouts of the lens in 2009 and discovered it had ended up in a private collection in Howell, Michigan, belonging to Steve Gronow, who operates the Maritime Exchange Museum.

Gronow explained that he bought the lens from the widow of the owner of Automatic Signal, the company hired to remove it in 1960 when it was converted to an automated light. Apparently, the Coast Guard official in charge gave the lens to her husband, and it remained in his collection until she sold it. Gronow offered both the Spring Point Ledge optic and another one from Michigan's Belle Isle Lighthouse for sale in 2009, yet neither sold at the time.

In 2018, a federal judge ruled in favor of the government and ordered Gronow to surrender both lenses to the Coast Guard. When they went to his mansion in Michigan to recover the lens in November 2018, Gronow refused to open the gates to his property to let them in. They returned to the judge, who ordered both lenses be surrendered to the Coast Guard by February 2019.

I contacted the Spring Point Ledge Light Trust to see if they were in possession of the original Fresnel lens or if they knew its whereabouts. According to the Trust, it was returned to the Coast Guard, and, as far as they know, it is currently at Connecticut College in New London, Connecticut. The organization continues working to return the Fresnel lens to Spring Point Ledge Light. ⚓

SPRING POINT LEDGE LIGHT

PORTLAND BREAKWATER LIGHT

Other Names: Bug Light
Location: South Portland
Tower Height: 25 feet
Focal Plane Height: 30 feet
Year Built: 1855, 1875
First Lit: 1855, 1875
Fog Signal: 400lb fog bell (1897), 1,000lb fog bell (1903)
Past Optics: Lamps and reflectors, sixth-order Fresnel lens (1855)
Present Optic: 250mm
Range: 9 nautical miles
Characteristics: Flashing white every 4 seconds
Year Automated: 1934
Year Deactivated: 1942 to 2002
Status: Active aid to navigation, city park
Keepers: W.A. Dyer (1855 – 1857), William L. Willard (1857 – 1860, died in service), Benjamin F. Willard (1860 – 1861), Benjamin Walton (1861 – 1866), Levi Strout (1866 – 1867), Paul McKenney (1867 – 1875), Stephen Hubbard (1875 – 1887, died in service), Albus R. Angell (1887 – 1900), Parker O. Haley (1900 – 1908), William A. Stetson (1908 – 1909), William T. Holbrook (1909 – 1919), Preston L. Marr (1919 – 1933).

Visit: This lighthouse can be viewed from land and is located at Bug Light Park in South Portland. The grounds are open but the tower is closed.

Portland Breakwater Light original wooden tower, c. 1859, USCGHO.

HISTORY

A terrible storm hit Portland Harbor in November 1831, destroying many buildings, wharves, and ships. A survey conducted in 1833 by the Army Topographical Engineers recommended building a 2,500-foot breakwater to avert large waves and make the harbor safer. Construction of the rubblestone breakwater began in 1836 and ended in 1838 when funds ran out for the project. It measured 1,800 feet long, and it was decided no more funds would be appropriated for further breakwater construction since it was already over budget.

The original plans called for a beacon at the end of the breakwater, but with the project already over budget, it wasn't built. Despite being shorter than planned, the breakwater did a good job of protecting the harbor, although mariners complained it was more of a hazard as it couldn't be seen in the darkness and heavy fog.

It wasn't until 1853 that the Lighthouse Board recognized the need for a small light to mark the end of the navigational hazard, which was nearly under water at high tide and extremely difficult to see and avoid on dark nights. The breakwater also made the channel very narrow, with vessels needing to pass between it and Hog Island ledge, making entering the harbor at night very dangerous. In 1855, a small wooden lighthouse was

Portland Breakwater Light early view, n.d,
Library of Congress.

constructed, and a sixth-order Fresnel lens was placed in the lantern room. A wooden keeper's dwelling was built on shore, although the exact year it was built is unclear. Many lightkeepers lived in their own homes nearby.

The original breakwater plans called for it to be topped with smooth ashlar capstone to make the surface even. Some of the breakwater had been capped, but not all of it, making many sections uneven and dangerous to walk across. Lightkeepers had to be careful during super high tides when the spray would crash over the breakwater, and it was nearly impossible to cross when the rocks were covered in ice in the winter.

In 1866, Congress approved funding to extend the breakwater an additional 400 feet. However, Col. J.D. Graham of the Army Corps of Engineers, who was in charge of the project, died suddenly, causing the project's postponement. His successor, Brevet Brigadier General B.S. Alexander, decided to conduct his own survey of the project, which caused further delay. Alexander was replaced by Lt. Col. George Thoms, who got the unfinished sections of the breakwater capped in 1868.

The breakwater was finally extended in 1873, making it a total of 1,990 feet long, and the wooden tower was moved to the end of the extension. In 1874, Congress approved funds to build a new lighthouse to replace the original wooden lighthouse.

Portland Breakwater Light close-up showing a column and
the decorative palmettes, n.d., Library of Congress.

The new lighthouse plans are the most unique in Maine and among all lighthouses in the world. The design resembles the Choragic Monument of Lysicrates, located near Athens, Greece. This was the first use of the Greek Corinthian column style on the outside of a structure.

Like the Athens monument, the new lighthouse, completed in 1875, was cast iron and had six Corinthian columns placed equally around the outside. The edges of the roof and gallery deck were decorated with palmettes, which are ornamental radiating petals resembling the fan-shaped leaves of a palm tree. The original tower was moved to Little Diamond Island to be used as a lookout tower for buoy tenders.

In 1879, the light was changed to flashing red to make it distinguishable from boat lights in the harbor and other lighthouses in the area. It

PORTLAND BREAKWATER LIGHT

wasn't until 1880 that a 58-foot handrail was installed at the lighthouse entrance to make moving around the lighthouse in inclement weather easier. In 1886, the handrail was extended the full length of the breakwater to the shore. In 1889, it was decided to build a small keeper's dwelling attached to the lighthouse so the dangerous crossing could be avoided, which consisted of only two rooms.

In 1892, a fuel house was built. In 1896, a 400-pound fog bell with an electric striking mechanism was added to the lighthouse. Around 1898, for reasons unknown, the light and bell were no longer being used, although they resumed in June of that same year. In 1899, a Stevens striking machine replaced the electric machine for the fog bell. In 1903, a 1,000-pound bell replaced the smaller one, and two more rooms and an attic were built onto the keeper's dwelling.

Portland Breakwater Light early view, n.d., USLHE.

Preston Marr, the last documented keeper at Portland Breakwater Light, retired on September 1, 1933, due to disability. After his retirement, the station was "under the charge of an additional keeper," although who that other keeper was is unknown. They would have served only until June 30, 1934.

In 1934, the lighthouse was electrified and operated remotely by the nearby Spring Point Ledge Light keepers. The keeper's dwelling and shed were removed from the lighthouse in 1935. In 1940, the water on the right side of the breakwater was filled in to create more land for shipbuilding, leaving only 100 feet of the breakwater out in open water. No longer a navigational hazard, the lighthouse was deactivated in 1942.

The lighthouse and property were eventually sold to a private party, and in 1985, Al Glickman of Spring Point Associates donated it to the city of South Portland. The South Portland Rotary Club and Spring Point Ledge Light Trust came together in 1989 to restore the lighthouse, which was relit as a private aid to navigation on August 14, 2002, featuring a new 250mm optic to replace the sixth-order Fresnel lens.

Portland Breakwater Light showing the external clockwork weight shaft that rotates the lens. It had to be outside because the lighthouse was too short to keep it inside, n.d., USLHE.

PORTLAND BREAKWATER LIGHT

The filled-in land is now owned by the city of South Portland and is known as Bug Light Park. In 2001, a Liberty Ship memorial was built in the park, representing the 274 ships built on the site throughout World War II. Most of the ships built there were Liberty Ships, which were used to carry supplies across the Atlantic during the war.

STORIES

The Marr Family

Preston L. Marr was the last documented keeper at Portland Breakwater Light from 1919 to 1933. He was born in 1871 at Hendricks Head Light, the son of Jaruel and Catherine Marr. His older brothers Wolcott H. and Clarence E. Marr were also lightkeepers, and Preston served as assistant to both of them at Cuckolds Light. Preston started as an assistant keeper in 1898, around the age of 27, and continued as a lighthouse keeper until he developed a disability while at the Portland Breakwater Light and could no longer work. He passed away two years later in 1935, around the age of 64, living most of his life in lighthouses.

The Holbrook Family

Portland Breakwater Light undated early view, possibly 1930s, Library of Congress.

William T. Holbrook was keeper of Portland Breakwater Light from 1910 to 1919. He lived there with his wife and older son Elias, his wife Florence, and his daughter Grace. The couple had two more children while living at the lighthouse: William (Bill) and Raymond (Ray). Ray Holbrook wrote down many of his memories of the lighthouse as a child, which are now kept at the South Portland Historical Society.

Ray remembers the harshness of the winters the most. He wrote that sometimes the window in the dwelling would break during storms, letting in the cold air and ocean spray. A stove in the kitchen was the only source of heat, and they would stand next to it to get dressed. He remembered how "dangerous" it was to use the

outhouse, which had shafts that went into the water below. The wind would blow up through the shafts during high tide, so they were sure to check the tides before going out to use it.

He remembered watching horse-drawn sleighs crossing over the ice to nearby islands in the winter. One of Ray's most memorable moments at the lighthouse occurred on November 11, 1918. At 11:00 a.m. that day, every boat and factory in the area blew their whistles to celebrate the end of World War I. ⚓

PORTLAND BREAKWATER LIGHT

HALFWAY ROCK LIGHT

Other Names: Half-Way Rock Light
Location: Casco Bay, South Harpswell
Tower Height: 76 feet
Focal Plane Height: 77 feet
Year Built: 1871
First Lit: 1871
Fog Signal: 1,000-pound bell with striking apparatus (1887), Daboll fog trumpet powered by diesel engines (1905), currently automated horn, 2 blasts every 30 seconds
Past Optics: Third-order Fresnel lens
Present Optic: VRB-25 solar-powered
Range: 19 nautical miles
Characteristics: Flashing red every 5 seconds
Year Automated: 1975
Year Deactivated: n/a
Status: Active aid to navigation
Keepers:
Head: John T. Sterling (1871 – 1883), George H. Toothaker (1883 – 1885), William T. Holbrook (1885 – 1890), Charles S. Williams (1890 – 1891), J. Harmon Stover (1891 – 1893), Parker O. Haley (1893 – 1900), Edmund Coffin (1900 – 1902), John B. Dewyea (1902 – 1921), Wesley Gray (1921 – 1934).

First Assistant: Joseph Edwards (1871), James T. Jones (1871 – 1872), Horatio G. Cook, Jr. (1872 – 1873), William J. Whitehead (1873), George H. Toothaker (1873 – 1883), William T. Holbrook (1883 – 1885), George H. Small (1885), James W. Sterling (1885 – 1887), Paul A. Durgan (1887 – 1888), Eli M. Alexander (1888 – 1889), Isaac W. Morrison (1889), J. Harmon Stover (1889 – 1891), Edmund Coffin (1891 – 1900), John B. Dewyea (1900 – 1902), Walter S. Adams (1902 – 1904), Giles H. Farley (1904 – 1907), William H. Burns (1907 – 1912), Roger P. Philbrick (1913), Fuller E. Larrabee (1913 – 1916), Wesley Gray (1916 – 1921), Ned R. Murphy (1921 – 1922), Evander W. Murphy (1922 – 1926), Everett E. Moore (1926 – 1929), Arthur R. Stevens (1929), Arthur S. Strout (1929 – 1934), John L. Pendell (1934 – c. 1936), Hoyt W. Cheney (1935 – 1942), William A. Clark (c. 1937 – c. 1939).

Halfway Rock, before 1889, NA.

Halfway Rock, after 1889, USCGHO.

Second Assistant: John D. Wight (1871), Albert F. Purrington (1871 – 1872), Sylvanus E. Doyle (1872 – 1873), Willis E. Chase (1873), P.G. Drinkwater (1873 – 1874), Albert F. Purrington (1874 – 1881), Theo B. Purington (1881), William T. Holbrook (1881 – 1883), George H. Small (1883 – 1885), James W. Sterling (1885), Isaac W. Morrison (1886 – 1889), J. Harmon Stover (1889), Edmund Coffin (1889 – 1891), Oliver P. Burns (1891), Edward H. Pierce (1891 – 1892), John B. Dewyea (1892 – 1900), Benjamin F. Henley (1900), Frank L. Peabbles (1900 – 1902), W.L. Curtis (1902), Walter S. Adams (1902), John L. Dyer (1902 – 1904), Giles H. Farley (1904), Leroy S. Elwell (1904 – 1907), Harold Hutchins (1907 – 1908), Thomas L. Godfrey (1908), John C. Morong (1908 – 1909), B.S. Rollins (1909 – 1910), Eugene W. Osgood (1910 – 1912), Roger P. Philbrick (1912), Albert J. Clinch (1913), Wyman M. Larrabee (1913 – 1914), Wesley Gray (1914 – 1916), Andrew J. Griffin (1916), William Foster Reed (1916 – 1920), Ned R. Murphy (1920 – 1921), Evander W. Murphy (1921 – 1922), Martin Sabins (1922 – 1923), Augustus S. Kelly (1923 – 1926), E.E. Moore (1926), Bernard A. Small (1926), Arthur R. Stevens (1926 – 1929), Arthur S. Strout (1928-1929), C.J. Wheeler (1929), Howard A. Ball (1929 – 1932), John L. Pendell (1932 – 1934), G. Duffy Brown (1934 –).

Coast Guard Keepers:
Officers in Charge: Arthur S. Strout (1934 – 1945), Archie W. McLaughlin (1945), Wilbur Brewster (1945 – 1948), Louis J. Nagy (1948 – 1949), Norman Goben (1949), Stephen F. Flood (1949 – 1950), H.N. Robinson (1950), John P. Sawsha (1950), William L. Lockhart (1950 – 1951), John L. Mason (1951 – 1952), James R. Seward (1952), Leon G. Lewis (1952 – 1953), Forrest S. Cheney (1953 – 1955), James R. Wilson (1955 – 1956), Harry L. Cressey (1956 – 1957), Michael A. Stern (1957 – 1958), James E. Murray (1958 – 1961), Leon E. Minzy (1961 – 1962), James E. Murray (1962 – 1966), Horace A. Leverett (1966), Chester E. Nichols (1968-1969), Richard F. Alexander (1969- c. 1970), D.J. Bestwich (1970 -), Stephen Krikorian (– 1975).

Assistant Coast Guard Keepers: Albert F. Osgood (1940– c. 1942), Hoyt W. Cheney (1943 – 1944), Reuben Kurtti (1947), Julian Hatch (1950 – 1951), William Yost (c.1951-1952), Evan Lavigne (c. 1953), Bradford S. Nelson (c. 1953), Harry S. Easton (c. 1954), Thomas Hunter (c. 1954), Carl Salonick (- 1954), Julian C. Lavigne (1954-), James F. Gormley (1954-), Laurier Burnham (c. 1957), Carl Bergeron (c. 1960), Wayne O. Armas (c. 1959-1960), Robert T. Hedrick (c. 1959-1961), Karl L. Bergeron (c. 1959-1961), John Cluff (c. 1960), Kenneth Rouleau (1960 – 1961), John Clough (c. 1961), Donald G. Barnes (1961-1962), Lloyd F. Manning (1961-1962), John W. Cluff (1961-1962), Walter A. Dodge (1962), Leon E. Minzy (1962), Danny L. Harris (1962), S.V. Cousins (1962-1963), Gerald H. Guay (1962-1963), Chester L. Baker (1963), Wayne F. Davis (1963-1964), Joseph J. Davis (1963-1964), Steven V. Skaw (c. 1964), Edward O'Shea (c. 1966), Robert R. Shillace (c. 1966), Edward Hannula (c. 1966), Joseph F. Smith (c. 1967-1968), James M. Kane (-1968), E.C. Warren (- 1968), August A. Pfister (1968), Tarling (1968-1969), Daniel J. Fortin (c. 1968-1969), Edward L. Williamson (c. 1968-1969), Richard Shuman (1969 – 1970),

Halfway Rock, 1942, USCGHO.

HALFWAY ROCK LIGHT

Munger (1969-1970), J.W. Ward (1969-1970), Samuelson (1970-), Clinton Jackson Jr. (1970-), Dave Gaspar (c. 1971), Frank Reese (c. 1971), Timothy Bailey (1971-1972), Lawrence E. Johnson, Jr. (early 1970s), Thomas Kuznicki (early 1970s), Stephen Krikorian (c. 1975), Ken Field (early 1970s), Ronald A. Handfield (c. 1975), Larry Caron, Jr. (c. 1975).

Visit: Both the lighthouse and grounds are closed to the public. Sea Escape Cottages & Charters out of Bailey Island offers tours that pass by Halfway Rock Light.

Halfway Rock keeper, boat, & laundry, July 1952, William Frederick Yost, Ford Reiche Collection.

HISTORY

Halfway Rock got its name due to its location, roughly halfway between Cape Elizabeth and Cape Small in Phippsburg. It took many shipwrecks, lives lost, and written requests from locals and high-ranking officials before congress would finally approve the construction of a lighthouse on one-acre Halfway Rock. It was a total of 36 years from the start of petitioning to when the lighthouse was built.

The lighthouse took two years to build. The initial cost estimate was too low, and construction was halted when the funds ran out. More funds were appropriated for the project, although the weather and labor shortages caused significant construction delays.

The first light finally shone on Halfway Rock on August 15, 1871, and the optic in the lighthouse was a third-order Fresnel lens. The granite blocks used to build the lighthouse were dovetailed together for additional strength so the lighthouse would withstand the fierce winds and violent waves that would crash into the island during storms. A stone boathouse was also built on the rock along with a long boat slip.

Halfway Rock, 1953, USCGHO.

Unlike most other light stations, there was no keeper's house. Those tending the light lived inside the lighthouse, making this a "stag" station, and families had to live nearby on the mainland. The lighthouse was divided into five levels. The kitchen was located on the first, the head keeper lived on the second, two assistants lived on the third, a watch room with a stove and a desk was on the fourth, and the fifth level was the lantern room.

In 1887, a 43-foot tall wooden skeleton bell tower was bolted to the ledge and housed a 1,000-pound bell with a mechanical striking mechanism. The construction of the bell tower proved solid that winter when a rough storm covered the rock in eight feet of water at high tide.

A wooden boathouse measuring 18 by 24 feet with a two-bedroom loft was built in 1889.

Coast Guard tender approaches Halfway Rock, 1960, Kenneth Rouleau, USCG.

It was bolted to the ledge and tower on the lee side of the lighthouse and had a wooden ramp leading down to the water. While the additional living space helped relieve some stress of close living quarters, during storms the only safe place to be was inside the lighthouse.

An 8-foot square wooden oil house was built and placed on top of a 20-foot high wooden frame that was bolted to the ledge in 1890. There were complaints by mariners that the fog bell wasn't enough during bad weather and limited visibility. In 1905, it was replaced with a diesel-powered Daboll fog trumpet. The station received electricity in 1936. A radio beacon was added in 1945 to further assist mariners in navigating the dangerous area.

In February 1972, a bad winter storm damaged the Fresnel lens, and the Coast Guard decided to automate Halfway Rock Light, which was completed in 1975. In 2004, Halfway Rock Light was declared one of the state's "Ten Most Endangered Historic Properties" by Maine Preservation. It fell into a state of disrepair due mainly to the fact that the location itself, combined with the weather, made landing on the rock difficult, therefore prolonging restoration efforts.

In 2012, Halfway Rock Light was made available to a qualified custodial organization, yet none came forward to take on the task of maintaining the lighthouse. In 2014, the lighthouse was put up for auction to the general public and was sold for $283,000 to Ford Reiche from southern Maine. He restored what was once on Maine's 10 Most Endangered Historic Properties list, the lighthouse and dwelling, to what they looked like in the 1950s. Reiche created a website, halfwayrock.com, which shows images of the restored lighthouse and dwelling, and also wrote a book about the history of the lighthouse and documents the restoration efforts that went into restoring the lighthouse and dwelling.

Halfway Rock aerial view, August 2017, Jeremy D'Entremont.

STORIES
Halfway Rock Wrecks
Shipwreck of the *Samuel*
On June 19, 1835, the merchant vessel *Samuel* was sailing north to Bath when gale-force winds came in from the southeast. Captain George W. Small was a veteran of the sea and knew the area could be dangerous in these conditions, although, instead of seeking a safe harbor and waiting out the winds, he chose to continue on the route. He had the crew reef the mainsail (reduce the size of the sail) with the intention of riding out the heavy winds further offshore where there is less risk of running into ledges. Unfortunately, his plan failed, and the captain and crew lost control of the ship.

Captain Small realized the ship was on a crash course with Halfway Rock, and in a last-ditch effort, he and his steward were wrestling with the jib boom when a rogue wave washed over the ship, taking both men with it, never to be seen again. The ship struck Halfway Rock around 10 pm that night. The remaining crewmembers were able to get to safety on Halfway Rock and took shelter among the ledges as the waves crashed over them and the small island throughout the night. The following morning, they were rescued by fishermen from Hope Island.

Shipwreck of the *Boadicea*

British barque *Boadicea* left New Orleans on December 2, 1860, and was en route to Glasgow, Scotland. On February 12, 1861, massive amounts of wreckage washed ashore on Jewell and Inner Green Islands, just three miles inland from Halfway Rock. Those who went out to search the islands for crewmembers found nothing more than deck planking, other wooden fragments of the ship, and a severely destroyed medicine chest with the faint words "Boadicea" on it. The crew had not seen Halfway Rock, most likely because it becomes completely submerged in times of rough seas, high winds, and high tide. They crashed into the rock at full speed, and all aboard perished.

Halfway Rock Light, 2017, Dave Wright, USLHE.

Arthur Strout and Willaim Clark

The Fight for Refrigeration

In the 1930s, the lighthouse crew at Halfway Rock Light petitioned heavily for a refrigerator. Refrigerators were only given to stations where families lived, and since this was a stag station, the need to keep food cold was deemed unnecessary. The crew was finally given a refrigerator in 1937, and they removed some shelves in the galley pantry so it would fit. Keepers Arthur Strout and William Clark signed and dated the back wall to mark the monumental occasion, which can still be seen there today.

Hidden Protest

When Washington D.C. announced that the U.S. Lighthouse Service would be disbanded and the duties and positions transferred over to the U.S. Coast Guard by 1939, there was much anxiety and unhappiness among lighthouse keepers. Many keepers were not happy that the Coast Guard's way of life was being forced upon them. When a deteriorating wall in the living quarters of the Halfway Rock lighthouse was removed during restoration in 2016, owner Ford Reiche found a whiskey bottle left in the wall dated "Xmas 1938" and signed by Arthur Strout and William Clark. Liquor was not allowed on the premises, and so the men most likely drank the whiskey in protest of the upcoming changes and placed it inside the wall for future generations to find and get a good laugh out of it! ⚓

The bottle of whiskey left in the wall by Strout and Clark, 2016, Ford Reiche.

ADDITIONAL PHOTO CREDITS

PHOTO CREDIT ABBREVIATIONS

USCG- United States Coast Guard | **USCGHO**- United States Coast Guard Historian's Office | **NA**- National Archives
USLHS- United States Lighthouse Service | **USLHE**- U.S. Light House Establishment | **USLS**- U.S. Lighthouse Society
ALF- American Lighthouse Foundation | **NPS**- National Park Service

PAGE	PHOTO LOCATION, DATE, CREDIT
Front Cover	Portland Head Light, n.d., [thomas] / Adobe Stock
Back Cover	Spring Point Ledge Light at sunet, n.d., [P.Meybruck] / Adobe Stock
Map	First L.H. Disctrict Map, Andrew B. Graham Photo Ltd., June 30, 1897, NA
1	Arctic Tern on a buoy near Hendricks Head Light, n.d., [rabbitti] / Adobe Stock
19	Whaleback Light, n.d., [alwoodphoto] / Adobe Stock
20	Small inset photo of finial on Cape Neddick Lighthouse lantern galley, 2010, Jeremy D'Entremont
20	Bottom, Cape Neddick, n.d., [joegoetz] / Adobe Stock
24	Aerial view of Cape Neddick Lighthouse, n.d., [Wangkun Jia] / Adobe Stock
25	Bottom, Boon Island Light, n.d., [Jeff Dobbs] / Adobe Stock
36	Goat Island at night, 2021, Dave Zapatka, USLHE
43	Wood Island Light, n.d., [thomas] / Adobe Stock
45	Aerial view of the Cape Elizabeth Lights, n.d., [Wangkun Jia] / Adobe Stock
59	Portland Head Light, n.d., [thomas] / Adobe Stock
64	Ram Island Ledge Light, n.d., [thomas] / Adobe Stock
68	Spring Point Ledge Light, n.d., [thomas] / Adobe Stock
72	Portland Breakwater Light, n.d., [SeanPavonePhoto] / Adobe Stock
Appendix A	Whaleback Light with Wood Island Light Saving Station in the background, n.d., [Jason] / Adobe Stock

APPENDIX A: ADDITIONAL PHOTO CREDITS

REFERENCES

All Among the Lighthouses, Mary Bradford Crowninshield (1886) [book], D. Lothrop & Company, Boston, MA.

Bangor News, Thirty-Three Years of Life Walking 'Round and 'Round, F.W. Keene, September 1, 1938.

The Century Magazine, Heroism in the Lighthouse Service: A Description of Life on Matinicus Rock, Gustav Kobbe, June 1897, p. 219-230.

Chronology of Aids to Navigation and the United States Lighthouse Service (Truman R. Strobridge)
    https://media.defense.gov/2020/Feb/28/2002256603/-1/-1/0/USLHS_CHRON.PDF

Find A Grave: https://www.findagrave.com/

Island Ad-Vantages, Burnt Coat Harbor light shines again, January 26, 1979, Brenda Lunt.
    https://archives.uslhs.org/sites/default/files/documents/Burnt%20Coat%20Harbor%20_0.pdf

The Keeper's Log, Volume XXIX, Number Two, Seguin Light Station, Maine, Jeremy D'Entremont, 2013.

Landscape Archaeology at the 1604-1613 French Settlements on St. Croix Island, Maine (USA), Steven R. Pendery (2010).
    https://www.academia.edu/5337335/Landscape_Archaeology_at_the_1604_1613_French_Settlement_on_St_Croix_Island_2010_

Lewiston Evening Journal, Sailor's Strange Dream Foretold Famous Maine Shipwreck, Frances Emery-Waterhouse, March 19, 1966.
    https://news.google.com/newspapers?nid=1913&dat=19660319&id=xHogAAAAIBAJ&sjid=rmcFAAAAIBAJ&pg=1029,2014316&hl=en

Lewiston Journal, Boyhood at Burnt Coat Harbor Light, November 12, 1977, Lucille S. Bangs.
    https://archives.uslhs.org/sites/default/files/documents/Lewiston_Evening_Journal_Sat__Nov_12__1977_.pdf

Lewiston Journal, Isolated Light Keepers on Maine Coast Maintain Lonely Vigil, David L. Sparks, January 5, 1957.
    https://archives.uslhs.org/sites/default/files/documents/isolated.pdf

Lewiston Journal, Story of Hendricks Head Light, September 16, 1933. https://archives.uslhs.org/sites/default/files/documents/1933.pdf

Lighthouse Digest Magazine, various articles/authors: http://www.lighthousedigest.com/index.cfm

Lighthousefriends.com (Kraig Anderson): https://www.lighthousefriends.com/index.html

The Lighthouse Keeper's Wife, Connie Scovill Small (1999) [book], The University of Maine Press, Orono, ME.

Lighthouses of Maine, Bill Caldwell (1986) [book], Guy Gannett Publishing Co., Portland, ME..

The Lighthouses of Maine- Acadia Region and the Bold Coast, Jeremy D'Entremont (2013) [book], Commonwealth Editions, Carlisle, MA.

The Lighthouses of Maine- Kennebec River to the Midcoast, Jeremy D'Entremont (2013) [book], Commonwealth Editions, Carlisle, MA.

The Lighthouses of Maine- Penobscot Bay, Jeremy D'Entremont (2013) [book], Commonwealth Editions, Carlisle, MA.

The Lighthouses of Maine- Southern Maine and Casco Bay, Jeremy D'Entremont (2013) [book], Commonwealth Editions, Carlisle, MA.

Lighthouses of the Maine Coast and the Men Who Keep Them, Robert Thayer Sterling (1935) [book], Stephen Daye Press, Brattleboro, VT.

Maine Lighthouses- Documentation of Their Past, J. Candace Clifford, Mary Louise Clifford (2005) [book], Cypress Communications, Alexandria, VA.

Maine Registry of Deeds: https://www.maineregistryofdeeds.com/

MEWreckChasers.com - Aviation Archaeology in Maine: http://www.mewreckchasers.com/closure.html

National Park Service: https://www.nps.gov/articles/a-very-roosevelt-christmas.htm

New England Lighthouses and Coastal Attractions: https://www.nelights.com/#gsc.tab=0

New England Lighthouses: A Virtual Guide (Jeremy D'Entremont): http://www.newenglandlighthouses.net/

Storms and Shipwrecks of New England, Edward Rowe Snow (1943) [book], Yankee Publishing Company, Boston, MA.

Tragedy on Matinicus Rock, Martin A. Siebert, 2006.
    https://www.scribd.com/document/321268672/matinicus?secret_password=PLbLujddLxBWD1sL2EGK#

United States Coast Guard History:
    https://web.archive.org/web/20170501202418/http://www.uscg.mil/history/weblighthouses/LHME.asp

United States Lighthouse Society: https://archives.uslhs.org/

US Lighthouses: https://www.us-lighthouses.com/

Wikipedia- Lighthouses of Maine: https://en.wikipedia.org/wiki/List_of_lighthouses_in_Maine

Wreckhunter.net: https://wreckhunter.net/newrecks.htm

YouTube, Nash Island Light: "Jenny's Island Life," https://www.youtube.com/watch?v=fbwTd5METSM and "Nash Island Sheep," https://www.youtube.com/watch?v=xyMdNf_0MTM

~FAIR WINDS AND FOLLOWING SEAS~